VINTAGE
ADVERTISING

VINTAGE ADVERTISING

AN A TO Z

JULIE ANNE LAMBERT

Bodleian Library
UNIVERSITY OF OXFORD

To my mother, Pauline Wilson,
and my husband, Keith Lambert

First published in 2020 by the Bodleian Library
Broad Street, Oxford OX1 3BG
www.bodleianshop.co.uk

ISBN: 978 1 85124 540 6

Text © Bodleian Library, University of Oxford, 2020
All images, unless specified, © Bodleian Library, University of Oxford, 2020

Cover design by Dot Little at the Bodleian Library
Designed and typeset by Laura Parker in 9.5 on 14.3 Ideal Sans
Printed and bound in China by C&C Offset Printing Co. Ltd
on 157gsm Chinese GS matt art paper

British Library Catalogue in Publishing Data
A CIP record of this publication is available from the British Library

CONTENTS

ACKNOWLEDGEMENTS

With special thanks to Michael Twyman, Alison Madden, Andrew Chapman, Rob Banham and Keith Lambert for their help in preparing the text.

SIX FOOTBALLS
GIVEN AWAY WEEKLY

INTRODUCTION

Advertisements are fun, engaging and imbued with the spirit of their age. All the more evocative for being chance survivals, they are simple and immediate in their appeal, and the detailed textual and visual information they provide is often not available elsewhere.

Whether we are interested in wines, sauces and pickles available in the 1840s (p. 121), the fashion for patterned hosiery in 1898 (pp. 102–3) or the appearance of the first Baird televisions in the early 1930s (p. 119), advertisements provide us not just with contemporary images or descriptions, but also with documents designed to sell – documents imbued with the most powerful means of persuasion the manufacturer or retailer had at their disposal.

Advertisements show us not just the product in question but also the preoccupations and anxieties of the consumer: Daniel Collins's 'Leather Straps & patent chains to prevent Trunks &c being cut from behind carriages' (p. 120), for example, or the actress Ellen Terry's assurances that '"KOKO" for the hair … stops the Hair from falling out' (p. 33).

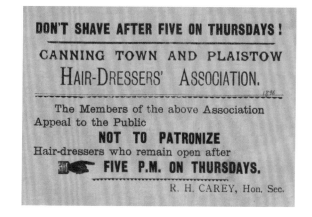

FIG. 1
Although not strictly an advertisement, this handbill (dated in manuscript to 1896) is interesting as evidence that small traders organized themselves into associations, with rules. Who can say whether this attempt to boycott those who contravened 'established' trading times was successful?

Detail of Newball & Mason advertisement (p. 54).

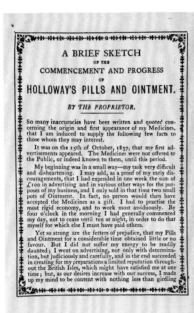

A BRIEF SKETCH
OF THE
COMMENCEMENT AND PROGRESS
OF
HOLLOWAY'S PILLS AND OINTMENT.
BY THE PROPRIETOR.

So many inaccuracies have been written and quoted concerning the origin and first appearance of my Medicines, that I am induced to supply the following few facts to those whom they may interest.

It was on the 15th of October, 1837, that my first advertisements appeared. The Medicines were not offered to the Public, or indeed known to them, until this period.

My beginning was in a small way—my task very difficult and disheartening. I may add, as a proof of my early discouragements, that I had expended in one week the sum of £100 in advertising and in various other ways for the purposes of my business, and I only sold in that time two small pots of Ointment. In fact, no person would then have accepted the Medicines as a gift. I had to practise the most rigid economy, and to work most assiduously. By four o'clock in the morning I had generally commenced my day, not to cease until ten at night, in order to do that myself for which else I must have paid others.

Yet so strong are the fetters of prejudice, that my Pills and Ointment for a considerable time obtained little or no favour. But I did not suffer my energy to be readily daunted; I went on advertising, not only with determination, but judiciously and carefully, and in the end succeeded in creating for my preparations a limited reputation throughout the British Isles, which might have satisfied me at one time; but, as our desires increase with our success, I made up my mind to be content with nothing less than girdling

the Globe with Depôts of my remedies. For this purpose I used to go down to the Docks to see captains of ships and passengers sailing to all parts of the world, collecting from them such information as was necessary.

It was a rule with me from the commencement to spend judiciously all the money I could spare in publicity, which went on increasing, until, in the year 1842, when I expended about £5,000 in advertising. Time rolled on, and from the hitherto unthought-of yearly outlay of £5,000 I increased it to £10,000 in the year 1845. At the time of the Great Exhibition in London in 1851 my expenditure was £20,000 per annum; in the year 1855 the cost of publicity had risen to the sum of £30,000; and in the present year (1863) it has reached £40,000, in advertising my Medicines in every available manner throughout the globe. For the proper application of their use I have had most ample directions translated into nearly every known tongue—such as Chinese, Turkish, Armenian, Arabic, Sanskrit, and most of the vernaculars of India, and all the languages spoken on the European Continent. Among my correspondents I number Kings and Princes, equally with other distinguished foreigners of all nations.

When the Ambassadors from Siam visited London in 1857, they were not only the bearers to me of an autograph letter from their *Major* King, but also of a gold enamelled ornament which they delivered here, arriving in one of the Queen's private carriages with a Prince Interpreter, who informed me, on the part of the Ambassadors, that this honour was paid to me as a testimony of his Majesty's satisfaction on learning that my remedies were introduced into his dominions, and with marked benefit to many of his subjects. The Ambassadors ordered at the same time, for his Majesty's use, Five Pounds worth of my Pills and Ointment, which were sent to their Hotel (Claridge's), Brook Street, Grosvenor Square.

(Signed) THOMAS HOLLOWAY.

244, STRAND, LONDON,
January, 1863.

Thomas Holloway

FIG. 2

In this 'brief sketch', Thomas Holloway elaborates on his advertising strategy – 'to spend judiciously all the money I could spare in publicity'. The escalating figures and his desire to advertise in 'every available manner throughout the globe' make Holloway a veritable pioneer of global marketing.

Some insights into the past are unexpected, challenging our preconceptions. It is perhaps logical that trunk-makers made coffins as well as knife boxes, but it might surprise us that they conducted funerals (p. 120). Renting a cooker from the Gas Office is also an unfamiliar concept today (p. 40).

There are occasionally items that puzzle us: the stark admonition not to shave after five on Thursdays (fig. 1) is intriguing, even though its message is clear.

Advertising was deemed essential by nineteenth-century entrepreneurs. Few speak so eloquently of its benefits as Thomas Holloway, manufacturer of patent medicines (fig. 2). Despite a spell in a debtors' gaol after overspending on advertising in his early career, the proceeds of his advertising-led business enabled him to found Royal Holloway College and Holloway Sanatorium.

CONTEXTS

We are used to seeing vintage advertisements out of context. If they are arranged at all (by a collector, for example) they might be organized by theme, genre or manufacturer but, typically, such recontextualizations assemble items from different periods and places.

What we cannot do is recreate their original context or view advertisements through the eyes of contemporary consumers. They were intended to jostle with one another on billboards, to provide striking splashes of colour as insets bound into journals (pp. 68–9) or to be distributed as handbills on the streets (fig. 3) — always vying for attention with their competitors.

That advertisements are redolent of their age is indisputable, but recreating a precise chronology for them is problematic. Their dates are usually elusive. The very immediacy of their message, the fact that their only context was 'now' and that they were not meant to survive means that very few advertisements are dated. Some may carry a printer's code or have been dated in manuscript by a helpful collector. There may be a similar advertisement in a dated journal or an obvious historic context (a war, coronation, jubilee, etc.) but very often there is nothing at all. Of the 98 items in this book, only 24 bear a printed date; of the others 14 have been dated in manuscript and a further 11 reflect a notable historic event that

FIG. 3
Handbills were one of the most powerful means of advertising. Millions were handed out on the streets and at railway stations in large cities, and tossed into cabs and carriages. Some were posted to targeted recipients, while others were distributed as 'insets' through journals (pp. 68–9). The 'hidden image' style of puzzle pictures was popular and had the advantage of retaining the attention of the viewer.

dates them precisely. The dating of the remainder required research. We have only to consider the advertisements which we glance at and recycle almost daily today to see the scope of the problem for future historians of our own period.

Nevertheless, the ability of advertising to encapsulate the zeitgeist (p. 136) enables us to see very clearly the evolution of the role of women, or changes in health products, domestic appliances and leisure pursuits, etc. There is a world of difference between the bored, pale mistress surveying her bonny servant spring cleaning on her knees (p. 108) and the emancipated cyclist (p. 28), just as there is between the mother in the Harlene advertisement who assumes that life for her daughter will be a replica of her own (p. 64–5) and 'Miss Remington' with her independent means of income (p. 131).

WAYS AND MEANS

The story of advertising is inextricably linked to the evolution of commercial illustration and art, and to changes in printing techniques and paper manufacture.

Advertisements form part of the wider genre of 'printed ephemera' (documents which were usually discarded after use). The necessity of making an impact meant that they were often at the cutting edge of developments in printing. Typographic ornaments, bold and ornamental typefaces (pp. 120–3), large woodcut illustrations and different coloured inks used mainly for playbills and posters for entertainments such as circuses, were appropriated by some early advertisers of commercial products. Such graphic means were perfect for arresting the attention of the passer-by in the street. Effective use of them was made in the 1820s by competitive lottery agents (p. 98).

During the second half of the nineteenth century, the mechanization of box-making and of cutting and folding paper and card enabled loose goods to be contained and subsequently branded. Before trademarks were formally established in 1875, the marks of authority on packaging, such as signatures, warnings against counterfeits and (sometimes) an integral government duty stamp (p. 92), were critical in providing a guarantee of authenticity. It was very common for an illustration of the packaging to be included in a manufacturer's advertising as an aide-memoire.

Paper-cutting techniques also led to the proliferation of novelties such as pop-ups, flaps and volvelles (pp. 60–61, 86–7) and die-cuts (pp. 40, 92–3, 105, 126). In common with less intricate giveaways, these novelties were produced to encourage the retention of the brand name.

ILLUSTRATION AND ART

Early (monochrome) illustrations in advertising were largely introduced to convey information. Early trade cards depicted trade signs and products (p. 120). Later, the premises themselves were often illustrated by engravers or lithographers on trade cards, bill headings or paper bags, etc. Such images can be invaluable sources for local historians. The trade card for E.F. Greenwood in St Giles, Oxford, for example, shows a building which no longer exists (p. 78), and there are many examples which record premises that have been demolished or modified.

The very novelty of an invention meant that it was frequently essential to explain and depict it in advertisements, often with the use of diagrams. George Keith, for example, makes use of illustration to show his new devices for making ice and ice-cream and for chilling wine in 1851 (p. 50).

The proliferation of catalogues from around the time of the Great Exhibition created a large and continuing demand for jobbing engravers and lithographers to illustrate subtly different products with sufficient accuracy for the customer to be able to make a choice between them. Although this was skilled work, such illustrations were rarely signed and were not considered as art.

It was the commercialization of chromolithography (pp. 36–7) with the introduction of powered machines from the late 1860s that revolutionized advertising, turning the monochrome (or near monochrome) printed world into an astonishing display of colour. The 1890s saw the birth of a British style of commercial art, whose exponents were free to unleash their imaginations on posters (p. 99) and advertisements for products from the banal to the latest 'must have'.

A MIRROR OF SOCIETY?

It is often claimed that advertisements mirror society, but the issue is complex. Most reflect the lifestyles and preoccupations of the well-off, if not the affluent. The Huntley & Palmers illustration of a children's party (p. 109 and detail opposite, in which the lines, dots and other marks characteristic of chromolithography can be clearly seen), for example, shows the inculcation of entitlement from a tender age.

The extent to which we can rely on the veracity of illustrations of domestic interiors (pp. 51, 64–6), children's clothes (pp. 29, 86, 93) or servants' uniforms (pp. 39, 84, 86, 108–9) is difficult to estimate, but we can assume that, while advertisers sought to enhance the beneficial effects of their products, there was little point in falsifying the wider context in which they were shown.

Women were the subject of the majority of illustrations in advertisements as well as being their intended audience. Through these images and the accompanying text, we can gain invaluable insights into the evolution of attitudes to womanhood, especially to upper-class women. They were perceived and used by advertisers in various ways: as mothers, as mistresses of households, as leisured wearers of fashionable attire or as fragile beings bolstered by a variety of health products. Until the 1890s, women were nearly always shown in their domestic setting, with their smiling, more robust servants or with their children (but rarely their husbands). If these images are stereotypes, they nevertheless reveal to us the aspirations of the age

Detail of Huntley & Palmers' advertising card (p. 109).

and the perceived or received ideals of beauty, of body contours, fashion, complexion, hairstyles, accessories and contextual decor. Advertisements also chart the gradual emancipation of women and the concomitant changes in dress, hairstyles and (above all) lifestyles (pp. 130–31).

By the 1890s most advertisements echoed posters (and indeed many were reproductions on a small scale of billboard posters). Ostensibly, there was little text to impair the effect of the image. However, unlike posters, advertisements afforded ample opportunity to promote and describe products by judicious use of the verso (the reverse side). When we follow the instruction to 'Please turn over' we return to the world of verbosity, of testimonials and of overstated claims more often associated with earlier advertising. While the front of the Matchless Polish die-cut advertisement (p. 105), for example, is devoted to celebrating the reign of Queen Victoria and promoting home industry, the verso carries an important warning to ladies: 'Metal polish that contains fatty acids will, when brought in contact with Brass, Copper, Zinc, &c., develop a most dangerous and poisonous copper compound better known as Verdigris, which ruins your brass and other metals, and spoils your hands.' Unsurprisingly, Matchless polish is guaranteed to be 'free from acid, poison or grit'.

It is through patent medicine advertisements that we are made aware of the suffering endured by those who could not afford medical treatment and of those who bought and were duped by quack medicines. Notorious for their exaggerated claims, such 'puffs'

not only listed a vast range of ills (cured by the same remedy), but often enumerated the distressing symptoms of disease. The newspaper advertisement of 1733 for Worm-Plaister (p. 60), for example, describes the many sufferings occasioned by worms.

Later advertisements also occasionally portray the sick, before and after treatment. The Mother Seigel's advertisement (p. 62) quite literally glosses over the sick man in the background, seemingly transformed by the syrup into the rotund cigar-smoking John Bull figure in the foreground. The woman suffering from a cold gains our empathy, and our envy when her cold is apparently cured instantly by the Carbolic Smoke Ball (pp. 60–61).

If the function of advertising was to sell by suggesting or portraying the advantages of the latest invention or fashion, advertisers of the eighteenth and nineteenth centuries did not try to sell a dream. The rising middle classes of the mid-nineteenth century, with their increased spending power, were often offered inferior versions of upper-class clothing, accessories and domestic items, promoted in low-quality advertisements and catalogues, on poor-quality paper and with few (if any) illustrations. Companies such as E. Moses and Son and the Borough Cloth Mart (p. 123) kept prices low by selling for 'ready money' rather than the credit traditionally extended to the rich. Customers could not overreach themselves financially, and society was intolerant of debtors.

The text was often in doggerel verse. Here E. Moses and Son purport to address all ranks of society:

The peer may here select, direct, according to his will,
For self and his establishment, at half his olden bill;
His groom may clothe at three pounds five, his tiger one
    pound ten;
His coachmen, footmen, at same rate, and all his helping
    men.

While we might assume that few peers of the realm took advantage of Moses' cheap prices, the marketing ploy of addressing gentlemen as well as the poor elevated the establishment as much as did their magnificent premises. (A 'tiger' was a smartly liveried boy acting as a footman.)

There is little sign of the poverty associated with 'Dickensian' London in advertising, unless we include Focardi's famous sculpture *You Dirty Boy* (bought by the Pears soap company) and humorous depictions of urchins and tramps in need of a wash. Servants, ostensibly well fed, clean and happy, are usually shown using the latest cleaning product under the watchful eye of their mistress (p. 108). When the world of the poor does intrude into the affluent, comfortable world of publicity, it is shocking (as it was intended to be). The F. Allen & Sons portrayal of intemperance and poverty (p. 38) is a striking example, especially with its implication that transforming their own lives is within the power of the family.

While it is rare that advertisers refer to political unrest in peacetime, there are occasional glimpses: the price of bread in the wake of the Corn Laws, or the free trade debate in 1903, for example (pp. 95–6). The E. Moses and Son advertisement mentioned above evokes the political crisis of the day, before enjoining the reader to 'overboard throw politics'.

The Boer Wars are heavily represented in advertising. Lords Roberts and Kitchener were frequently portrayed as heroes. The situation was very different during the First and Second World Wars. Paper shortages put a temporary stop to lavish stand-alone advertising, and most posters were dedicated to recruitment.

The light-hearted juxtapositions in this book are designed to point up by contrast both the simplicity and the complexity of looking at advertisements divorced from their original context. Each advertisement encapsulates elements of its era, contributing a tiny piece of knowledge to the jigsaw of our past.

Detail of Raphael Tuck & Sons poster (p. 133).

The NEW M...
FOR SPE...

MORRIS MOTORS LTD.

RIS - OXFORD SIX
& COMFORT

OXFORD

A TO Z

Put this in your Scrap book.

It cost **£20,000** to produce the first editions, inclusive of **£2,200** for the original painting.

"Bubbles" by Sir John E. Millais. Bart. R.A.

A perfect facsimile in miniature.
The original is in the possession of Messrs. Pears.

ART

The 1880s and 1890s witnessed an unforeseen and controversial fusion of advertising and fine art: manufacturers, notably A. & F. Pears and Sunlight Soap (owned by Lord Lever), saw the potential of buying existing paintings and using them to promote their products and enhance their status. Although the trend was not limited to soap manufacturers, the popularity of washing as a theme in fine art meant that relevant paintings were easily sourced.

In 1887 the art world was outraged by the transformation of John Everett Millais's *vanitas* painting *A Child's World* into the ubiquitous *Bubbles* – the *vanitas* tradition evoked the transitory nature of life through the use of symbols, notably here the bubble. A bar of soap and the Pears brand name were added to the painting as well as the new title. Millais did consent to this use of his painting, ostensibly because of the quality of the chromolithographic reproduction. Pears made much of the cost not only of acquiring the painting but also of the initial reproductions, as can be seen here. It was subjected to many further versions, not all as faithful to the original, in colour and in black and white. It was common practice to reproduce posters as wood engravings for monochrome journal advertising.

The proliferation of *Bubbles* on the hoardings must have been the first contact for many a working man or woman with the work of a Royal Academician, certainly in colour. From 1891 Pears devoted the supplements of their *Pears' Annual* to the dissemination in high-quality colour of (unadulterated) fine art, mostly by academicians, with the catchphrase 'A complete picture gallery for one shilling'.

Sunlight Soap caused further outrage in the art world in 1889 by transforming *A New Frock* by William Powell Frith, without the artist's permission, into the advertisement *So Clean*. This led to passionate debates about copyright and the threat posed by commerce to artistic integrity. The trend of appropriating fine art continued. Here we see the popular animal painter Charles Burton Barber's *Girl with Dogs* (c.1893) retitled *The Family Wash*, substantially altered and used as a Sunlight advertisement in c.1897, three years after the artist's death.

This genre of advertising coexisted with the emergence of an British school of commercial art, consisting mostly of academicians working outside their usual genres. The pioneers of this quintessentially British style included Henry Stacy Marks, Dudley Hardy and John Hassall (p. 56).

BICYCLES

Advertisers seized on the bicycle as a symbol of modernity, especially when ridden by women for whom bicycling was a means of liberation, enabling them to enjoy unaccompanied travel in the fresh air. It gave a strong message to society that some women at least were no longer prepared to be confined to the house and a life of dependence and inactivity. Producers of biscuits and certain beverages (including cocoa) marketed new and existing products for the refreshment of cyclists. Stower's lime cordial, 'free from musty flavours' (overleaf), styled itself in the 1890s as 'the only healthy beverage that can be safely taken after cycling or other exercise'. The cyclist's attire approaches in spirit that of the 'new woman' with her jaunty hat and daring show of ankle.

By the 1930s, cycling was commonplace and recreational rides into the countryside were enjoyed by both sexes, unencumbered by inappropriate dress. The geometrical and tonal abstraction of the landscape in this example and the strong zigzag line disappearing into the horizon are typical of the period.

STOWER'S LIME JUICE CORDIAL.
NO MUSTY FLAVOUR
ABSOLUTELY PURE and NON-ALCOHOLIC.
THE ONLY HEALTHY BEVERAGE THAT CAN BE SAFELY TAKEN AFTER CYCLING OR OTHER EXERCISE.
Carefully prepared from the Purest Refined Sugar and the Pure Juice of the Fruit. It forms a most eminently Healthy and Delicious Beverage, very Purifying to the Blood (*AND, THEREFORE, EXCELLENT FOR THE COMPLEXION*). See Medical Opinions.
SAMPLE FREE FROM ALL GROCERS,
WINE MERCHANTS, CHEMISTS, &c., THROUGHOUT THE UNITED KINGDOM.
PLEASE TURN OVER.

Norfolk Suit.
Very popular style for Boys from 6 to 14 years.
In Fancy Tweeds and Serges.
4/11 5/11 8/11
All-Wool Cheviots and Serges
10/9 13/9 16/9 19/9

Greenwich Suit.
Stylish Suit for Boys of 3 to 8 years,
in Tweeds and Serges.
3/9 3/6 4/6 5/11 6/11 8/11
Higher quality. 10/9 13/9 16/0

Parisian Suit.
High Class Suits for Boys 3 to 13 years,
made in Tweeds, Worsteds, and Fancy
Cloth—9/11 13/9 16/9 20/6 25/0
Also in Velvets, Brown, Navy Blue,
Black, and Claret
11/9 15/0 18/9 21/6 27/6

The Byron.
New and Effective Style in Tweeds
8/11 9/11 10/9

Highland Costume.
Full Dress.
Complete Costume, including Cap and
Hose—24/6 43/6 49/6
In Tweeds—10/9 14/9 16/9 21/6
Kilts in all Tartans—7/11
Inverness Cape Overcoats, to wear with
this Costume—9/11 11/9 15/9 19/9

Velvet Sailor Suit.
In Black, Navy, Brown or Myrtle
Velvets.
5/11 6/11 8/11 10/9 12/9
Superior Qualities—14/9 20/6 25/0
Special Line in Plush Suits, various
colours—8/11 10/9 11/9 12/9

CATALOGUES

Catalogues (which could be single sheets, leaflets or booklets) grew in importance as industrial expansion presented the consumer with an increasing choice of products. Illustration was essential, description alone being insufficient to differentiate models of cookers, grates, lawn mowers, knives, sewing machines, hats, etc.

Clothing catalogues, which usually portray the wearer, are among the most attractive, since they often indicate the domestic setting, pursuits, accoutrements and attitude of the targeted clientele.

The Fred Watts & Co. catalogue for 1896–97 epitomizes late-Victorian upper-class privilege. It includes a very limited selection of clothes for girls but focuses on boys, youths, men and servants' livery. Watts portrays his young male clientele in school wear for Eton and Rugby, sailor suits, formal dress and suits which emulate adult attire. The sketchy backgrounds throughout show the trappings of an affluent lifestyle. Unexpectedly among these is a tortoise: these exotic domestic pets were new in Britain.

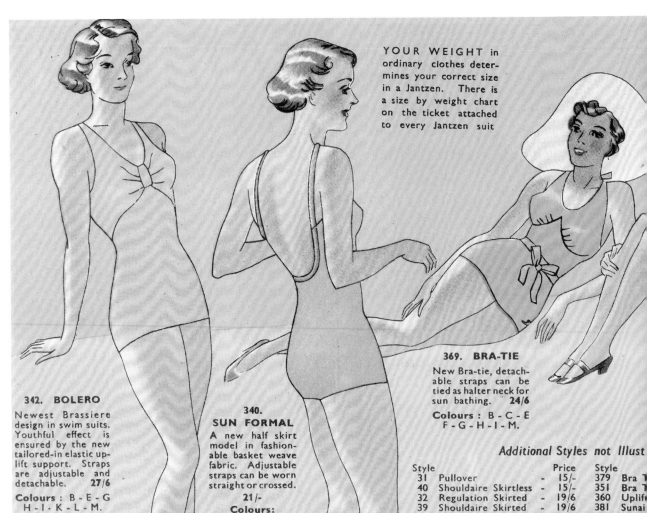

YOUR WEIGHT in ordinary clothes determines your correct size in a Jantzen. There is a size by weight chart on the ticket attached to every Jantzen suit

342. BOLERO

Newest Brassiere design in swim suits. Youthful effect is ensured by the new tailored-in elastic uplift support. Straps are adjustable and detachable.   **27/6**

Colours : B - E - G H - I - K - L - M.

340. SUN FORMAL

A new half skirt model in fashionable basket weave fabric. Adjustable straps can be worn straight or crossed.   **21/-**

Colours: B/C - E - F/C - H I - L/C.

369.   BRA-TIE

New Bra-tie, detachable straps can be tied as halter neck for sun bathing.   **24/6**

Colours : B - C - E F - G - H - I - M.

Additional Styles not Illust

Style		Price	Style	
31	Pullover	- 15/-	379	Bra T
40	Shouldaire Skirtless	- 15/-	351	Bra T
32	Regulation Skirted	- 19/6	360	Uplif
39	Shouldaire Skirted	- 19/6	381	Sunai
370	Bra Mio Skirtless	- 19/6	310	Trous
371	Bra Tuck Skirtless	- 19/6	378	Silhou
375	Sun Burst Skirtless	- 19/6	362	Sun-B

BLACK(A)   BAHAMA(B)   WHITE(C)   SILVER(D)   BERMUDA(E) FRENCH ROSE(F) CC

ORONATION

...ll suit, skirtless,
...s-over brassiere
...ailored-in elastic
...port. In solid
...ing contrasting
27/6

...lours :
...l/C - B - E - H.

	Price
...s -	19/6
...d -	24/6
-	24/6
...s -	24/6
-	30/-
...less -	39/6
...d -	47/6

364.
SQUARE BACK

Brassiere top with
tailored-in elastic up-
lift support. A suit
for the slim and not
so slim. It has figure
control to a marked
degree.   27/6

Colours : A - B - E
G - H - K.

377. CHERIE
(With skirt style
37)
An interesting
new neckline,
cut to the waist
yet tailored to
fit modestly.
New elastic up-
lift support in
brassiere top.
Suit - 27/6
Skirt - 14/6
Colours :
B - C - D - E - I.

341.
SUNBURST

The new adjust-
able Sunburst
brassiere moulds
your figure in
beautiful lines.
Straps adjustable
and detachable,
can be tied as
halter neck. 24/6

Colours :
B - E - H - I - L - M.

(G)   CAPRI (H)   NAVY (I)   CARRIBEE (J)   PAGAN (K)   RIO (L)   MAIZE (M)

SPORTS SUITINGS

**Kynoch are famous for their Sports
Suitings Twists Cheviots Saxonies**

Only 40 years later, the Jantzen swimwear catalogue for coronation year (1937) demonstrates how the boundaries of acceptable dress had changed (pp. 30–31).

Kynoch's innovative marketing largely rescued the company (which was founded in 1788) from the effects of the Depression. Their 'loud', fun catalogues of the early 1930s captured the public imagination, associating the brand with outdoor pursuits such as golf and skiing, all accompanied by the trademark Scottish terrier. In reality, we know from a catalogue which incorporates fabric samples that the tartans and plaids were much more sober.

CELEBRITIES

The cult of showing images of celebrities in advertising began in the 1880s – an extension of the well-established practices of royal endorsements and testimonials, usually from doctors or professional men. Female celebrities were typically actresses and singers.

The actress Lillie Langtry gave her name to face powders and endorsed Harlene hair preparation, but was most closely associated with Pears' soap: 'Since using Pears' Soap for the hands and complexion I have discarded all others.' Pears also used endorsements from actress and singer May Fortescue, opera singers Marie Roze and Adelina Patti, and actress Mary Anderson.

'Koko for the Hair' was well served by testimonials from Ellen Terry over many years, with her famous

I Use KOKO FOR THE HAIR

Miss ELLEN TERRY, our Great Actress, writes:—
I have used "KOKO" for the Hair for years, and can assure my friends that it stops the Hair from falling out, promotes its growth, eradicates Dandriff, and is the most pleasant dressing imaginable

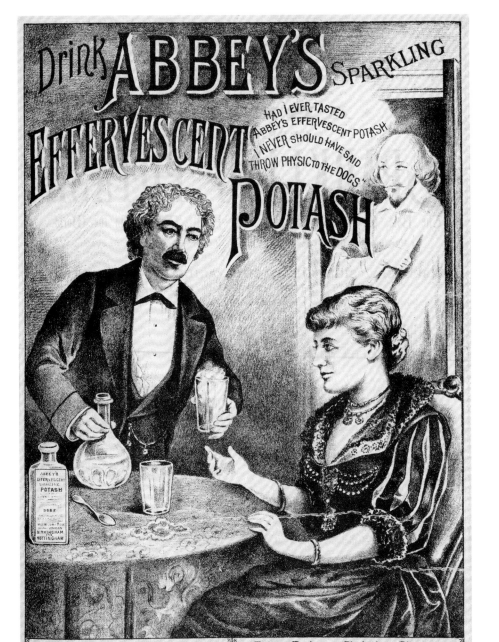

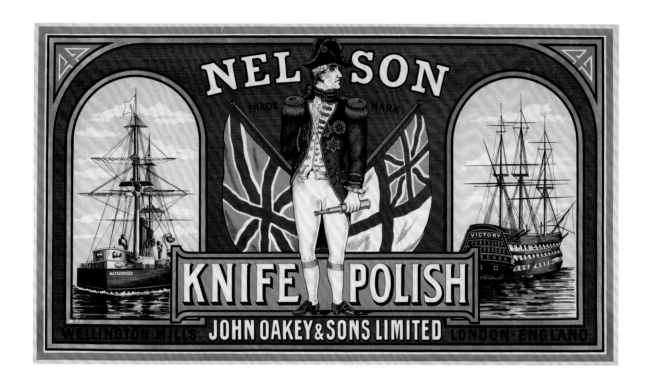

halo of untameable hair. A testimonial on the verso dates the use of the image to *c.*1896, when the actress was forty-nine.

The advertisement for Abbey's Effervescent Potash of *c.*1885 shown here is unusual in featuring Shakespeare's ghost alongside portraits of and testimonials by the famous English operatic tenor (John) Sims Reeves and the Swedish soprano Christina Nilsson. Shakespearian quotations were often taken humorously out of context to suggest the Bard's endorsement of products, e.g. 'For Soap –

Pears' (for so appears); here his shade suggests that the line from Macbeth (Act V, sc. III), 'throw physic to the dogs', would not have been written had the Bard known about Abbey's potash.

Male celebrities were thinner on the ground in advertisements, the explorer Harry de Windt's endorsement of Harlene's hair-restoring properties being a rare example. However, several products were named after military and naval men or carried images of them: Wellington hosiery, or the 'Duke of Wellington's tooth powder', for example. John

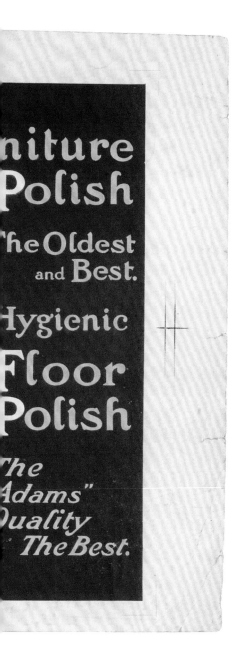

Oakey & Sons adopted Wellington's profile as their trademark and named their mill after him. They marketed both 'Wellington' and 'Nelson' knife polishes. The box label on p. 35 dates from the 1890s.

CHROMOLITHOGRAPHY

It would be difficult to overstate the impact of commercially viable colour printing, which brought colour to the hoardings and into the home in the last few decades of the nineteenth century. Many of the colour advertisements in this book were originally produced by chromolithography, which required the image and its text to be separated onto separate stones, drawn in reverse, one for each colour, and printed successively. This early twentieth-century proof retains its 'tablets', showing the number of colours and the order in which they were intended to be printed. Tones, in the form of dots, lines and other textures, were then applied to the otherwise flat colours. The rendering of the reflections is particularly fine.

COCOA AND CHOCOLATE

It is rare for poverty to be so starkly portrayed for commercial purposes as it was in this F. Allen & Sons' cocoa advertisement, which exploits the association of cocoa with the Temperance Movement (the most notable advocate of which was the Quaker Henry Rowntree).

This Cadbury's advertisement proclaims the nutritional and health-giving properties traditionally associated with cocoa, but goes further than most in its 'scientific' analysis of and support for cocoa's 'flesh-forming' (proteins) and 'heat-giving' (carbohydrates) qualities in relation to raw beef, mutton, eggs and white bread. The claims are backed up by medical and other journals. The charming image of a domestic scene in 1896 shows the benefits of cocoa to young and old. There is no suggestion that the nursemaid might also partake of the benefits of cocoa.

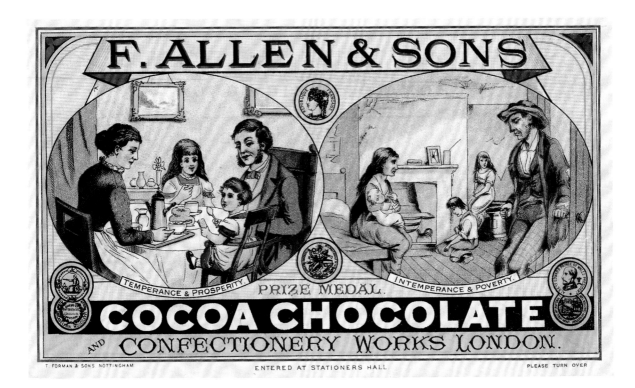

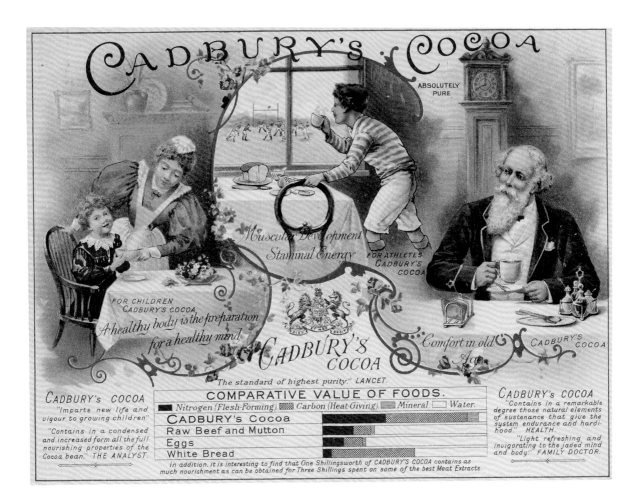

COOKERY ASSISTANTS

In the 1890s and early 1900s, demonstrations of the latest cookers became a form of entertainment. The provocatively dressed and coquettish cookery assistants (visually distinguished from servants by their white aprons and flat caps) drew the crowds. These two cookers use different fuels. The Eureka is marketed for the economy and cleanliness of gas in relation to coal ranges and clearly targets the poor, who would be tempted to rent rather than buy.

The Albionette oil stove advertisement of 1896 is reminiscent of Dudley Hardy's 'Yellow Girl' (p. 99)

THE "EUREKA" COOKER can be RENTED for a nominal Quarterly sum from the GAS OFFICE

Established 1871.
"Pioneers of the Oil Stove Industry"
THE
ALBION LAMP
COMPANY.
RIPPINGILLE'S.
ALBION LAMP COMPANY, BIRMINGHAM.
THE
"ALBIONETTE"
Dudley Hardy. 96.
our Latest and BEST.

(credited as the first poster in the British commercial art style) and features a jovial chef in addition to his assistant. The verso carries fascinating claims of the stove's capacity ('dinner parties of from six to twenty-five persons') as well as promoting its use on yachts, in shooting boxes and on military expeditions.

CORSETS

The pseudoscientific fad for electromagnetic devices in the 1880s–1900s led to the development of electropathic belts for both sexes and 'magnetic' or 'electric' corsets for women. The latter doubled as figure-enhancing and 'health-giving' aids, the claim being that they cured weak backs and a range of illnesses, such as dyspepsia (indigestion), kidney disorders and hysteria, without medicine.

Although corsets date from the fifteenth century, it was in the late-Victorian era that tight-lacing to achieve the desired hourglass figure threatened the health of the wearer by realigning organs and affecting the functioning of the lower lobes of the lung, the circulation, liver, uterus and gall bladder, as well as weakening muscles and causing back pain.

Even allowing for the touching-up of photographic images, the marketing of the 'Adjusto' in 1910 as a traditional corset for ladies of 'unusually generous proportions' is disturbing. The relative liberation offered by rubberized elastic girdles shortly after this date must have been a great relief.

Royal Worcester "ADJUSTO" Corsets
FOR GENEROUS OR FULL FIGURES.

This **Corset** can be worn by any Lady of unusually generous proportions, with luxurious freedom and comfort.

Consonant with the utmost regard for **Health,** the body is reduced by several inches, without any undue pressure or discomfort

Stock sizes 22 to 30 inches or up to 36 inches, at a slightly increased charge.

In Strong White Coutil · · · at **15/11**
Or of Superior Quality · · · ,, **21/9**

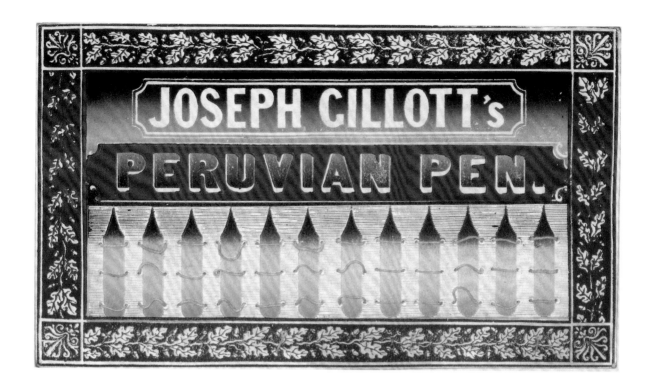

DISPLAY CARDS

Cards produced to display goods in shops needed to be eye catching and attractive to secure a sale. Joseph Gillott's Peruvian Pen card (c.1850s) makes use of the effect of rainbow printing, and would originally have had a full set of nibs. The Birmingham company, founded in 1827 and still in business today, specialized in the manufacture of steel pens and enjoyed royal patronage. Wynter Bros & Co. of Bradford applied for a trademark for a preparation for chapped hands in 1924. This display card contains a full set of the boxes, each of which contains a tablet wrapped in waxed paper and a folded advertisement.

45

"Grandma with Candles was lighted to bed,
Mamma says that she used Gaslight instead,
I have B.T.H. EDISON Electric Light,
Switched on and off by Nurse every Night."

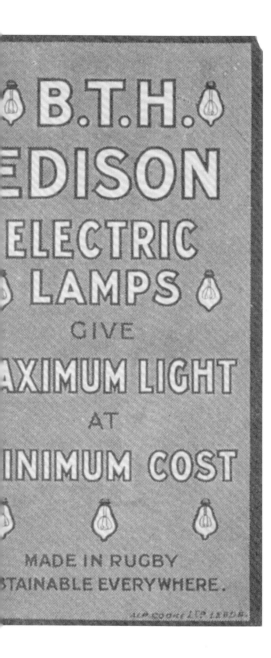

ELECTRICITY

Before the construction of the National Grid in 1933, electric lighting in homes was powered by various companies, with some experimental implementations as early as the 1880s. Domestic electricity was affordable only by the wealthy, epitomized by the girl in this advertisement whose family had clearly benefited from the latest lighting technologies, all of which were costly in their day. The advertisement shown here must date from *c*.1902, the year B.T.H. Edison began production in their newly constructed factory in Rugby.

The Ideal Home Exhibition was founded by Lord Northcliffe, proprietor of the *Daily Mail*, in 1908. The General Electric Company's 'Pavilion of Light' was an innovation for 1930 and reflected the public's enthusiastic adoption of the new electric appliances, which were to increase the comfort of their homes and save labour.

Demonstrating

the important part which lighting plays in the home, and to show its true relationship to architecture, furnishing and decoration.

The G.E.C. Pavilion of Light has been erected in connection with the £1,000 Competition organized by the "DAILY MAIL" in conjunction with The General Electric Co. Ltd. A suite of six rooms were open to competition; four to Architects—the Lounge, Dining room, Bedroom and Nursery—and two to electrical contractors—the Kitchen and Bathroom. The winning designs have been followed, and the rooms constructed, exactly as submitted, and they constitute a unique revelation of the ingenuity and resource of British craftsmen in devising novel and beautiful effects for the home in harmony with the modern spirit.

Other rooms of interest are Ariadne's Bath and garden lounge.

The whole of the illumination scheme for the Pavilion of Light has been carried out by The General Electric Co. Ltd.

"DAILY MAIL" IDEAL HOME EXHIBITION

G.E.C. PAVILION OF LIGHT

FOOD PRESERVATION

The preservation of food before refrigeration was a problem addressed by many enterprising manufacturers.

In his advertisement produced for the Great Exhibition of 1851, George Keith proposes a range of devices for making ice and ice-cream, cooling food and wine, and planing ice for sherry cobblers (cocktails of orange, sugar, sherry and crushed ice).

By contrast, this 1932 blotter and calendar, issued by the Gas Light and Coke Company, shows a modern, gas-fuelled kitchen which was promoted for its efficiency and economy, since only one servant was deemed necessary to run it.

"COME INTO MY KITCHEN—"

The gas equipped kitchen of today is the keystone of household health and comfort ... with gas for cooking, water-heating, warming, refrigeration and destruction of household refuse, one servant can do the work that needed three servants in an old fashioned house of the same size.

CALENDAR BLOTTER 1932

	APRIL				MAY				JUNE			
S	-	3	10	17	24	1	8	15	22	29	-	5	12	19	26
M	-	4	11	18	25	2	9	16	23	30	-	6	13	20	27
Tu	-	5	12	19	26	3	10	17	24	31	-	7	14	21	28
W	-	6	13	20	27	4	11	18	25	-	1	8	15	22	29
Th	-	7	14	21	28	5	12	19	26	-	2	9	16	23	30
F	1	8	15	22	29	6	13	20	27	-	3	10	17	24	-
S	2	9	16	23	30	7	14	21	28	-	4	11	18	25	-

With the compliments of the Gas Light and Coke Company

GIMMICKS

In 1884 A. & F. Pears overstamped a quarter of a million French 10 centime coins with the brand name Pears' soap. At this time, the coins were legal tender in Britain. During the First World War, some of the coins were supposedly found on the battlefields, enabling the company to re-exploit their original gimmick.

Aerial propaganda is usually associated with warfare rather than advertising, but George Philip Lempriere (1855–1949), balloonist and aeronaut, was a pioneer in advertising from the skies using balloons, kites and aerial banners. The novelty of this advertisement is twofold: not only was it 'dropped from the skies' (on 16 June, 1894), but it is printed on Japanese paper. More commonly used to commemorate events, Japanese paper souvenirs were usually produced in the square format of handkerchiefs. Whether Japanese or Western in style, the borders were pre-printed in Japan and subsequently overprinted with text in Britain.

A Message from the Clouds!!

DRINK

"PRIORY

TEA.

Best Value in the World!

INSIST ON HAVING IT
FROM YOUR GROCERS.

In Packets only.

1/2, 1/4, & 1/7 PER LB

Special Golden (Priory) Blend 1/10 per

THIS HANDBILL was dropped from the
skies by Lieut Lempriere, navigating
the "Golden Eagle" Balloon,
June 16th, 1894.

GIVEAWAYS

The free gift business took many forms. There were competition prizes, gifts in exchange for vouchers and a range of giveaways. To keep the brand name in the consumer's mind, manufacturers created a range of cardboard toys and games for children, and bookmarks, blotters, calendars and almanacs for adults. Collectibles, often in series, were inserted into packets (of tea, cigarettes, etc.) to encourage brand loyalty.

The Nottingham firm Newball & Mason's advertisement announces a competition for 'six splendid footballs for the six most interesting postcards' relating to Mason's coffee essence. The verso specifies that the content should be 'a good joke, a storyette, conundrum, puzzle, sketch – anything but a limerick'. The footballer is in the club colours of Notts County, known as the Magpies or Pies. Formed in 1862, they are the oldest professional league club in the world. Although undated, this handbill is likely to have been produced in 1894. The figure bears a striking resemblance to the Scottish footballer James Logan, who scored a hat-trick for Notts County in their FA Cup win against Bolton Wanderers that year. Logan died tragically young two years later at the age of 25.

The Bournville game of quoits (c.1903–5) features vignettes of the recreational facilities of 'A factory in a garden'. Bournville's utopian factory, which also boasted schools and parks, was a source of pride to Cadbury's, as were the healthy conditions under which their cocoa was prepared by British workpeople (referred to on the verso). The pin or spike over which the disc is normally thrown is replaced here by a cocoa 'tin' in cardboard. No opportunity was lost to reinforce the packaging in the consumer's mind (pp. 91–3).

HASSALL, JOHN

John Hassall's early posters did not achieve the international acclaim accorded to Dudley Hardy's, but it was his style which dominated the British scene for several decades, earning him the national accolade 'king of the poster'. He introduced a quintessentially British humour to the poster that was popular with the public and critics alike. The simplicity of his outlines meant that designs conceived as posters could be easily reproduced at smaller sizes – as handbills, postcards and the like. For ten years, he worked for the large poster company David Allen and Sons, creating entertainment, travel, political and advertising posters in the new British artistic style. Hassall's longevity (1868–1948) and his creation in 1900 of the New Art School in Kensington (superseded after its closure in the First World War by the John Hassall Correspondence Art School) meant that the broad basis of the style was perpetuated and taken up by a number of commercial artists, among them H.M. Bateman, Harry Rountree and Bruce Bairnsfather.

This postcard of 1924 reproduces one of Hassall's iconic posters as an advertisement for its publisher, J. Weiner.

HATS

In the nineteenth century, hats were worn by all classes of society – from gamekeeper to squire and from maid to mistress. Their structure, form and level of trim varied widely and fashions changed frequently. Advertisers had to convey not only the range of their products but their intended clientele. The somewhat fussy poster from *c.*1888 (overleaf) specifically designates the 'Model' bonnet as for the elderly while the 'Mildred' was for young ladies.

A disadvantage of hats was their inevitable exposure to weather. The washable beaver hat (*c.*1837) was an ingenious invention and a boon to those of limited means. Charles Dickens refers to 'washable beaver hats, that improve with rain' in *Oliver Twist* (ch. 37). The illustration is thought to be by George Cruikshank.

INVALUABLE DISCOVERY. NEWLY INVENTED

WASHABLE
Beaver Hat.

The above important discovery will be found an immense saving to Gentlemen, inasmuch as after the Hat has been worn and exposed to all kinds of weather for some time— it is easily restored to its original shape and beauty, by the simple process of WASHING. The Inventor offers them at a price which places them within the reach of the Public generally, and feels confident that persons once wearing them, will acknowledge the **Washable Beaver Hat** superior to all others. These Hats are of a brilliant and lasting colour, light and elastic, and the finest that can be produced.

Best Quality, in every variety of fashion for the Month. **19s. 6d.**

Superfine ditto, combining the same fashions . . . **17s. 6d.**

Inventor and Maker.—**PITT & Co.**

No. 4, King William Street,
WEST STRAND·

The Milton Press, 9, Chandos Street, Strand.

THE GERTRUDE.
Panama Sailor Hat, band of green velvet round crown, covered ecru lace, trimmed both sides with bows of white satin ribbon. Price **6/11** Postage 9d

THE DUCHESS BONNET.
Jet Bonnet, trimmed bow of lace across front, mauve lilac and black osprey, bows of satin ribbon at back and strings. Price **8/11** Postage 9d

THE
Pretty Gold tips, ribbon paste or

THE VENETIAN.
very pretty Heliotrope Straw Hat, trimmed with ch white satin ribbon bows at back, ivy foliage and bunch of osprey in front. Price **10/11** post free.

THE HAZLEMERE.
Panama Hat, band of ribbon velvet round crown, black tips at side, roses on brim and underneath at back, small paste ornament in front. Price **14/11** post free

THE AGNES TOQUE.
Pretty Toque made of green straw, cream lace and osprey at side, flowers, ribbon bow at back, loops of straw in front. Price **11/9** post free.

THE H
Jet Bonnet, tri match, jet bow back and ribbo Price **10/11** pos

THE MODEL BONNET.
Elderly Ladies' Bonnet, made of black lace, jet band round edge, trimmed tips and osprey, lillies of the valley in front, satin ribbon strings with bows at back. Price **14/11** post free.

THE CECILIA.
Panama Hat, band of black velvet round crown, prettily trimmed at side with white tips, satin ribbon and lace. Price **11/9** post free.

THE MILDRED.
Brown Straw Hat, for young lady, bows of satin ribbon and yellow flowers round crown. Price **7/11** Postage 9d

TH
Brown Fancy Straw green ribbon at side, and brim, fancy o

THE PICTURE HAT.
Lovely Gold Chip Hat, trimmed green and blue ribbon, spray of french roses at side with bunches of blade grass, ivy leaves on brim, and paste pins with coloured centres. Price **21/-** post free.

SPECIAL SALE OF ARTISTIC MILLINERY.

J. W. LEWIS, 193, 199, 200, 201, 202, Upper Street, LONDON, N.

HEALTH

While some nineteenth- and early twentieth-century patent medicine advertisements preyed on fear and listed alarming symptoms in the manner of the eighteenth century, others focused on the cure.

In this newspaper advertisement of 1733, the accompanying woodcut illustration shows a (presumably used) worm-plaister being handled with some distaste. Not only did Dr Higham's plaister cure the symptoms of worms, including stinking breath, gnashing of the teeth and convulsion fits, but the puff claims that it was efficacious against 'Cholick, Phthisick [pulmonary consumption], Shortness of Breath … Agues or Fevers'.

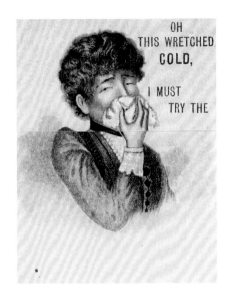

Dr. *HIGHAM*'s famous Worm-Plaister.

Applying it the Pit of the Stomach, immediately deſtroys all Sorts of WORMS in the Bodies of Men, Women and Children; gives preſent Relief in the Cholick, Phthiſick, Shortneſs of Breath, &c. is the only Arcanum in the World to cure Agues or Fevers, and is ſo innocent a Preparation, that you may apply it to the Stomachs of Children a Week old, or Women with Child may uſe it with Safety.

Perſons that are afflicted with Worms have commonly a ſtinking Breath, troubleſome Sleep, frightful and terrible Dreams, knaſhing of the Teeth, an itching and often picking of the Noſe, Convulſion Fits, a violent Head-ach, and many other Diſorders too tedious to mention; all which are inſtantly eradicated, and the Patients reſtor'd to their native Health and Vigour, by applying this excellent Plaiſter to the Pit of the Stomach. Sold at the Rainbow Coffee-houſe by Fleet-Bridge, price One Shilling with Directions.

N. B. No Perſons are ever troubled with Convulſion Fits or Falling Sickneſs, that uſe themſelves to this Plaiſter. 1733

MOTHER
SEIGEL'S
SYRUP

ONCE
"A VICTIM OF INDIGESTION"

NOW "ALWAYS MERRY & BRIGHT"

The flap advertisement on pp. 60–61 is a simple but effective method used by manufacturers to show 'before' and 'after' states. The Carbolic Smoke Ball Co. is famous for the court case relating to the £100 reward offered in 1891 to anyone who used their product but still got influenza. Louisa Carlill's claim to the reward was upheld in court. In 1893 the company increased the reward to £200, stating that only three people had been awarded the initial sum. However, they went out of business three years later. The advertisement dates from the early 1890s.

The Mother Seigel's advertisement of *c.*1900 is unusual in showing a sick man, albeit alongside his happier and healthier alter ego.

INTERIORS

Advertisements convey much information about contemporary interiors – graphic detail which it is difficult to obtain elsewhere, especially in colour. While homes might be idealized (especially in relation to the product being advertised) there was no reason for them to be falsified. Thus we see fashions in furniture, soft furnishings, floor coverings, windows, fireplaces, dado rails, light fittings, tiles, crockery, ornaments and much else.

Through the Harlene advertisements of *c.*1892 (pp. 64–5) we gain rare admittance to a lady's dressing room. Unusually, these two advertisements show contrasting decors, perhaps to reflect the seasons. The immutability of life as a woman in the Victorian and Edwardian eras is suggested by the little girl's assumption that she will follow in the footsteps of her mother in aspiring to a good head of long hair. Hair-cutting for women (as opposed to the styling of long hair) was in vogue from the 1920s (p. 102).

Hall's advertisement for distemper (p. 66) shows the new fashion for clean lines, simple furniture and lack of clutter of the early 1930s. The console radio in the corner, with its large but light wooden case, adds a technological dimension to the modern look.

"Mama, shall I have beautiful long hair like you when I grow up?"
"Certainly, my dear, if you use **'Edwards' Harlene'**."

"Mamma, shall I have beautiful long hair like you when I grow up?"
"Certainly, my dear, if you use **'Edward's Harlene'.**"

JOURNAL ADVERTISING

Journals and magazines played a crucial role in advertising. From at least the first half of the eighteenth century into the twentieth, journal wrappers carried advertising for books and products. Initially consisting just of the four pages constituting the cover, these 'advertisers' expanded into many pages of front and end matter. It was intended that they be discarded when the journal was bound. Where they survive, they provide an invaluable record of dated advertising, targeted at specific readerships. For example, the engraved version (overleaf) of this undated window bill (small poster) in the June 1889 issue of *Sunday at Home* enables us to date it.

The same image shows the way in which handbills (known in this form as insets) were distributed through journals. Sewn, stapled or glued (as here) within the monochrome pages, they provided colour and often superior printing.

4

THE RELIGIOUS TRACT SOCIETY, 56, PATERNOSTER ROW, AND 164, PICCADILLY, LONDON.

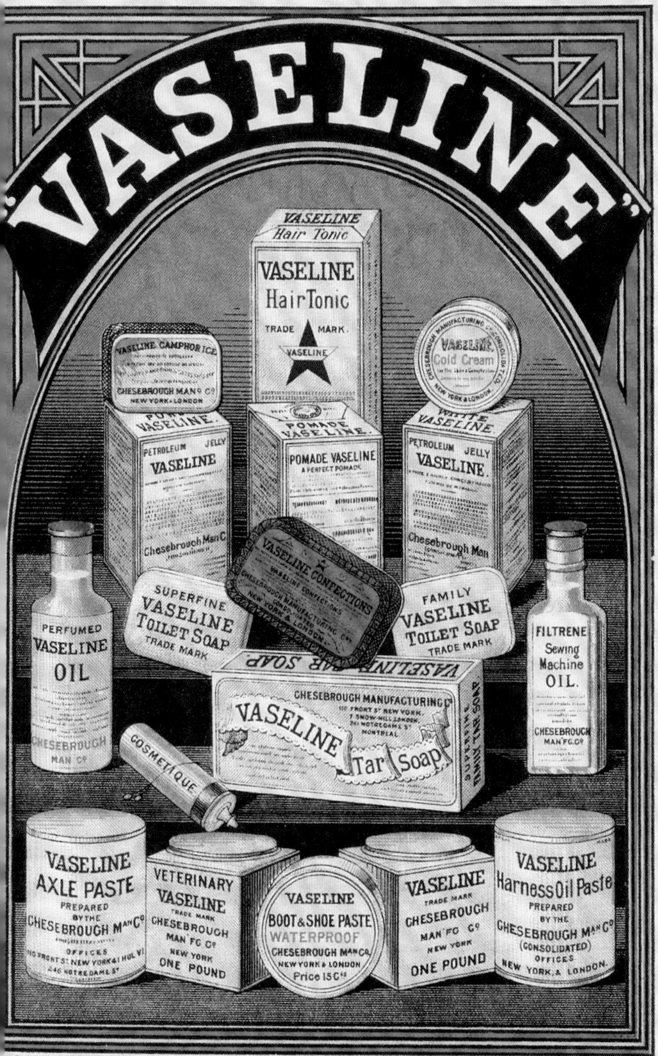

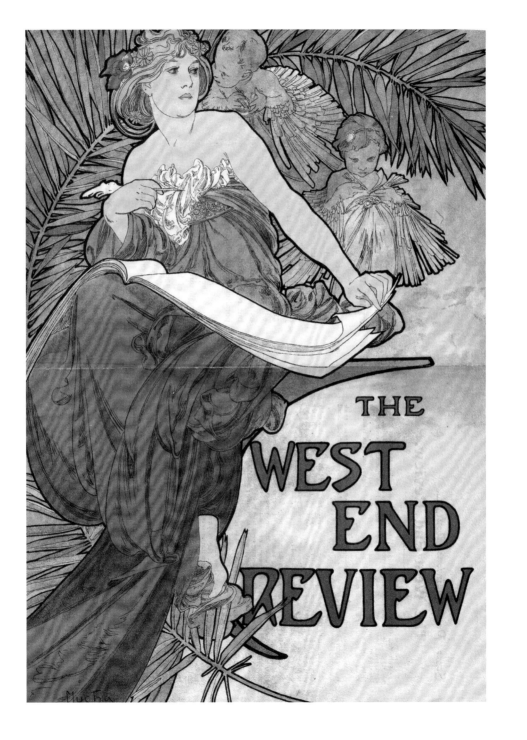

THE
WEST
END
REVIEW

The market for journals and magazines was very competitive and window bills, posters and prospectuses advertising them were often designed to a high quality by established artists. This art nouveau design for *The West End Review* by Alphonse Maria Mucha (1860–1939) was produced as a poster in nine sheets by Lemercier in Paris. It was used as a cover for the journal itself ('a new and striking cover in colours has been designed by a distinguished artist') and for this 1898 prospectus, printed by Harrison & Sons, 'Printers in Ordinary to Her Majesty'.

The striking prospectus for the new series of the *Pall Mall Budget* in 1890 is a reduction of a much-lauded poster by the English artist Maurice Greiffenhagen, RA (1862–1931).

KINGS

Queen Victoria's long reign was followed by a succession of kings. Their coronations provided an opportunity for advertisers to capitalize on royal imagery.

Lewis & Burrows (formed in 1895) deflected the glory of King Edward VII's coronation onto themselves in the graphically witty verso of their charming image of the forthcoming coronation: 'Lewis & Burrows … have already been crowned with success' (pp. 74–5).

Rowntree's coronation casket (1911), shown here, provides a useful photographic record of King George V and Queen Mary, the royal family and the empire.

The General Electricity Company's lavish brochure *Coronation Celebrations*, showing street lighting for the coronation of Edward VIII in 1937 (pp. 76–7), was all wasted effort as 'GR' had to be hastily substituted for the coronation of George VI in the same year.

· DEPENDENCIES ·   OF · THE · EMPIRE ·

· CORONATION · SOUVENIR · 1911 ·

· CANADA ·

GEORGE V. · H·M· QUEEN MARY.

· AFRICA ·

AT THE AGE OF 5 YEARS

MARLBOROUGH HOUSE

AT THE AGE OF 2½ YEARS

PRINCE JOHN.   PRINCE ALBERT.   PRINCE GEORGE.   H.R.H. PRINCESS MARY.

All loyal subjects are looking forward to the

CORONATION

OF OUR BELOVED

KING & QUEEN.

FE **1150** CORDISSE.

Illuminated circular shield, 5ft. 3ins. diam., finished as shown, and outlined with 15m/m red CLAUDGEN Neon tubing. Three circles of blue tubing, each 2ft. in diameter, are superimposed on the face of the panel. " E.R." 14-in. letters. With five 3-yard flags. Electrodes and transformer encased at back. Complete with all H.V. equipment for connection to any specified A.C. supply between 200 and 250 volts, 50 cycles.

Price   ..   ..   **£45   0   0** each

Approx. current consumption, 200 watts.
Other voltages and periodicities entail small extra charge.

FE *1151* COROJOY.

This effective device comprises a Plymax panel, 8ft. × 2ft. 6ins. overall, with illuminated outline of 15m/m blue CLAUDGEN tubing. " E.R." in 10-in. letters on 18 × 15-in. panel, illuminated from behind by red tubing. Electrodes and transformer encased at the back. With five 3-yard flags. Complete with all H.V. equipment for connection to any specified A.C. supply between 200 and 250 volts, 50 cycles.

Price .. .. **£38 10 0** each

Approx. current consumption, 150 watts.
Other voltages and periodicities entail small extra charge.

L

LOCAL HISTORY

Advertisements bear witness not only to the changing commercial use of buildings, but to the evolution (and sometimes the very existence) of the buildings themselves. Beyond the invaluable information provided by the addresses alone, illustrated trade cards, bill headings (invoices), paper bags and shop advertisements provide visual resources for local historians often unobtainable elsewhere. The building occupied until 1931 by E.F. Greenwood in St Giles, Oxford, for example, was demolished to make way for the extension to the Taylor Institution. A manuscript annotation dates this trade card to 1884. The verso shows the eclectic range of local British and foreign produce stocked by this 'Foreign fruiterer & Italian warehouseman, cook & confectioner'.

Landmarks and monuments that feature in advertisements sometimes also bear testimony to the past. The Brighton Aquarium was designed by Eugenius Birch and opened in 1872. The addition of its distinctive clock tower and gateway two years later dates this window bill to the mid- to late 1870s. The aquarium was extensively modernized between 1927 and 1929, and the tower was demolished.

BRIGHTON STEAM

BISCUIT COMPANY'S

AQUARIUM BISCUITS

MOTORING

Motoring began as the pastime of a privileged
elite and was gradually democratized by technical
improvements, the creation of more modest cars and
by the availability of hire purchase agreements. By
the 1930s, motoring brochures were curious hybrids:
part technical information, part alluring images. This
illustration from *The Book of the Riley Nine Plus Ultra
Series* for 1932 lifts to reveal details of standard colour
schemes and equipment, and of variations offered for
the chassis, wheels, wings and upholstery.

The New Morris-Oxford Six poster (overleaf) is
a pure expression of the 1930s love of abstract line,
conveying speed and liberation.

Monaco Half-Panel Saloon
("Plus-Ultra" Series)

MORRIS MOTORS LTD.
COWLEY OXFORD

The NEW MORRIS-OXFORD SIX
FOR SPEED & COMFORT

MORRIS OXFORD

THE MORRIS OXFORD PRESS LTD.   PRINTED IN GREAT BRITAIN

NOVELTIES

It is astonishing to find complex paper technology, which is usually associated with moveable books and Christmas cards, used in the service of a dairy company. The front cover of the exquisite pop-up image shown overleaf (p. 86) illustrates the delivery of milk, with rare images of contemporary milk receptacles, a milk cart and a milkman's uniform. The extent, layout and rural surroundings of College Farm, Finchley, are shown on the back cover. The pop-up image itself shows an affluent, obviously healthy household of seven children (one a baby with feeding bottle) and a cat, all nourished by milk under

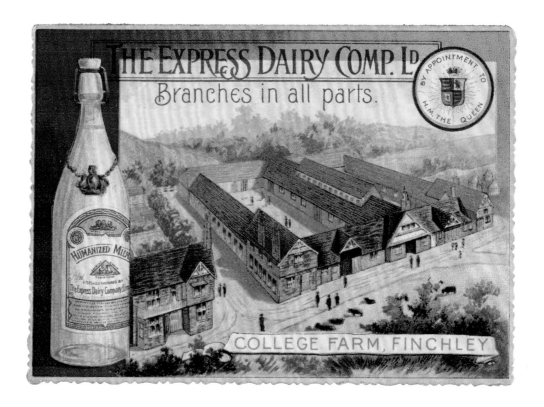

the watchful eye of their nursemaid. This was no ordinary dairy, however. Established in 1883 by George Barham (inventor of the milk churn) as a model dairy to promote hygiene, College Farm was open to the public daily. When an outbreak of cattle plague virtually wiped out urban cows in London, the Express Dairy Company delivered milk from the countryside, including (it would seem) to the royal household

Volvelles (or wheelcharts) bound into codices date back to the thirteenth century. Later examples enabled astronomical, chronological, navigational and other complex scientific calculations to be made by moving

the revolving parts. But in advertising, they were merely used as novelties. This 1890s 'peep show' reveals 'The world's great bridges': London Bridge, Forth Bridge, Clifton Bridge, Tay Bridge, Tower Bridge ... and Owbridge! Note the packaging carried by the little girl.

Such changing images were not unrelated to magic lantern shows or zoetropes: ways of conveying motion were being actively explored in this pre-cinema age.

OPTICAL ILLUSIONS

Hold-to-light advertisements were popular in the late nineteenth century and echo earlier transparencies, notably those published by William Spooner in the 1830s–1840s. Both relied on a light source to change the image: Spooner's were particularly elaborate, with substantial changes to scenery (such as the eruption of a volcano) achieved by broad washes of colour on the reverse following the contours of the printed and hand-coloured image. This later and simpler transformation advertising Brown & Polson's Corn Flour (*c*.1891) creates its effect by revealing a sailing boat, slogan and text printed in black ink on the verso. The spotlight effect and the 'audience' again reference the magic lantern shows of the pre-cinema age.

Pears produced many optical illusions: strobic circles which appear to revolve, and images which, if stared at for an extended time, change colour and migrate to blank spaces or become superimposed onto images of pears, seeming to ripen them. The 1887 optical illusion overleaf plays with the idea of scale and false perspective.

A POLITICOPTICAL ILLUSION !

Which is the greatest Statesman?

COPYRIGHT
[REGISTERED]

COPYRIGHT
[REGISTERED]

In the above Silhouette Churchill does not appear so tall as Salisbury, nor Salisbury so tall as Gladstone, but if measured they will all be found of equal height.

N.B.—No other equality is to be inferred.

PACKAGING

The advertisements on p. 91 and pp. 92–3 emphasize the importance of packaging in identifying products and protecting the consumer from counterfeits.

'I've got the right one' expresses the relief of the girl in this early twentieth-century Angier's advertisement who is in the act of comparing her purchase with the product shown in the poster. Although the placing of the poster seems improbable, hoardings were often set up in the countryside and caused much adverse comment, resulting in the formation of SCAPA (Society for Checking the Abuses of Public Advertising) in 1893.

The packaging in the 1898 Mellin's advertisement dwarfs the little girl and is reproduced in detail, including the Medicine Duty stamp across its top (such duty stamps were issued from 1783 to 1941). The advertisement opens to reveal a domestic scene of children ostensibly enjoying their cod liver oil. In the foreground is an enlarged bottle, on which even the directions are legible. The (rare) depiction of contemporary toys is a bonus to the historian of childhood.

THE NEW ESTABLISHED PATRIOTIC

CHEAP

BREAD

Manufactory,

No. 5, NEW STREET,

COVENT GARDEN.

Wm. FOWLER,

BAKER TO HER MAJESTY,

QUEEN CAROLINE,

Most respectfully invites the FRIENDS of REFORM and LOVERS of ECONOMY and RETRENCHMENT, to meet at the above Manufactory, every Day in the ensuing Week, to take into consideration the PRICE of BREAD; and for such a laudable Institution, the Subscriptions are so abundant, that the Establishment is now enabled to sell the very BEST BREAD, at EIGHT PENCE PER LOAF! and it is fully expected, from the very liberal Subscriptions already received, that shortly we shall be enabled to Sell the *BEST BREAD*, at *SIXPENCE PER LOAF!!!* and it is hoped that a generous Public will encourage so noble an Institution, by sending to No. 5, NEW STREET, for their Bread and Flour, and *no where else.* This will make the topping Baker come down, and, though reluctantly, say—

Of all the shops in Britain blest,
This is the cheapest and the best.

And the patriotic Baker will reply—

And whilst the times remain so hard,
Let others be upon their guard.

GOD BLESS THE QUEEN!

THE BEST BREAD NOW SELLING AT

No. 5, New Street, Covent Garden,

AT EIGHT PENCE PER LOAF.

Printed by W. GLINDON.   31, RUPERT STREET, Haymarket.

POLITICS

Some advertising ephemera is rich in political overtones, such as this handbill, which the reference to Queen Caroline dates to 1820-21.

In the wake of the Napoleonic Wars, during which imports from the Continent were blockaded, the Corn Law of 1815 was passed to prevent the import of foreign corn until British corn reached 80 shillings a quarter. Bread prices were artificially and disastrously high, leading to very real hardship. Here, William Fowler suggests that, by establishing a local monopoly, he will substantially lower the price of a loaf (loaves were four pounds in weight and called quarterns). The subversive references to Queen Caroline (especially 'God bless the Queen!') are testimony to her popularity with the masses. Estranged from and hated by her husband George IV, Caroline of Brunswick was nevertheless technically queen from January 1820, when he became king, until her death in August 1821. She returned from Italy to assert her right but was physically barred from the coronation on 19 July 1821. It scarcely matters whether she did, in fact, buy her bread from the Cheap Bread Manufactory.

This small poster (*right*) was issued by the pro-free trade paper the *Daily News* in November 1903. The graphic representation of the price of bread in relation to the relative wages and spending power of free trade and protectionist countries was intended to help the masses to understand the complex debate raging in the early twentieth century. The Board of Trade's 'blue book' on *British and Foreign Trade and Industry* was central to the tariff controversy.

FREE TRADE IN BOVRIL IS

PROTECTION

BOVRIL

AGAINST

COLDS & CHILLS

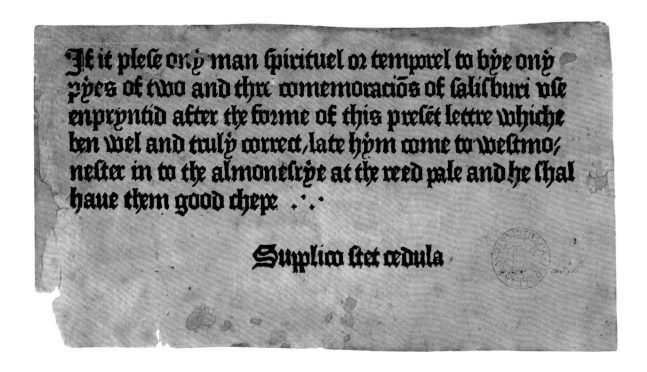

The Bovril advertisement celebrates the Liberal advocate of free trade, Sir Henry Campbell-Bannerman, who became prime minister in 1905 on the resignation of Arthur Balfour over the tariff controversy. CB, as he was known, won a decisive victory in the election of the following year.

POSTERS

We associate posters with large sheets, visible at a distance, but the essential defining element was that they were displayed or 'posted'. This makes William Caxton's c.1477 small advertisement for his own *Sarum Pie*, a handbook for priests, a highly significant document. It is both the first printed advertisement and the first printed poster in English. Wherever it may have been posted (possibly in a church porch), it was to be left in place (*supplico stet cedula*).

Lottery agents, fiercely competitive, were at the cutting edge of printed advertising. In the advertisement overleaf, woodcut illustration, large type (cut by hand) and printing in two colours are used for maximum effect. Such techniques were more usually associated with posters for entertainments.

Curiously, this poster for the last public lottery in 1826 omits the advertiser's name!

Jules Chéret, artist and (crucially) master lithographer, created his first artistic advertising posters at the very end of the 1860s in Paris, having found a way of making them effective on a commercial basis by using only four colours. It was more than twenty years later, in 1893, that Dudley Hardy's *Yellow Girl* poster for Jerome K. Jerome's *To-Day* magazine appeared on the billboards of London to great acclaim, heralding the foundation of a British school of commercial art. Although influenced by Chéret, British commercial posters differed both in technique and spirit. The British style was simpler, bolder and characterized by blocks of colour within strong black outlines. In the hands of Maurice Greiffenhagen (p. 71), the Beggarstaff Brothers (William Nicholson and James Pryde) and others, it was pared down even further. Many of the colour advertisements shown in this book must have been conceived and/or printed as posters. It was the poster that drew comment from the critics, the poster that was avidly collected, the poster that reached the masses on the rapidly proliferating billboards. Britain entered the poster scene just in time to be represented on the international stage, notably in journals, books, exhibitions and, significantly, in *Les maîtres de l'affiche*. This collection of small-scale chromolithographed facsimiles of the best posters, available by subscription, was printed under the expert eye of Chéret. The *To-Day* poster (seen here) was plate 216.

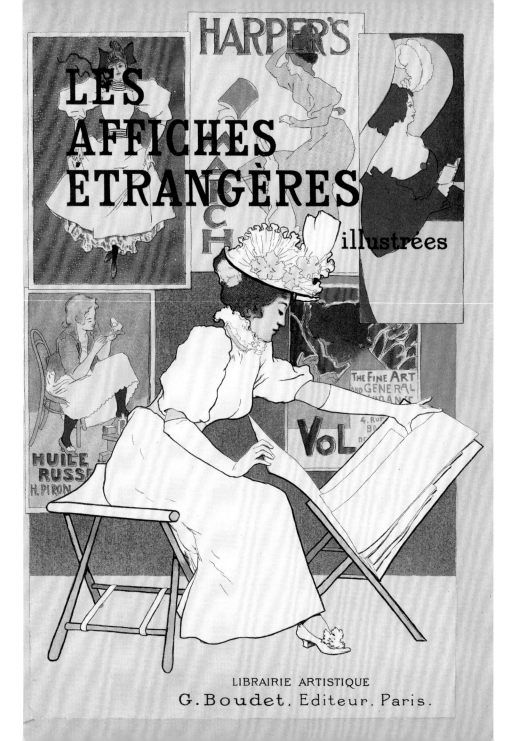

LES
AFFICHES
ÉTRANGÈRES

illustrées

LIBRAIRIE ARTISTIQUE
G. Boudet, Éditeur, Paris.

The beautiful upper wrapper of *Les affiches
étrangères illustrées* (Paris, 1897) includes a
representation of one of Dudley Hardy's posters
for the *Gaiety Girl*.

After the First World War, the gently humorous
style epitomized in Britain by John Hassall (p. 56)
was challenged by designers with a more abstract
approach, such as Edward McKnight Kauffer in this
1933 poster for Shell.

PRICES

Advertisements, and in particular catalogues, often include prices, but this jaunty 'circular' from 1898 for Bradbury, Greatorex and Co.'s patterned and embroidered hosiery is more innovative than most.

Although, for pragmatic reasons, some women cut their hair during the First World War, short hair was all the rage in the 1920s. Hairdressers, used to styling long hair, had to adapt their techniques to the new fashions. This handbill promotes the latest styles, with prices. Marcel waving (with heated tongs) was invented in the 1870s, but was originally applied to long hair. 'Eugéne' refers to Eugene Suter who essentially invented the 'perm'.

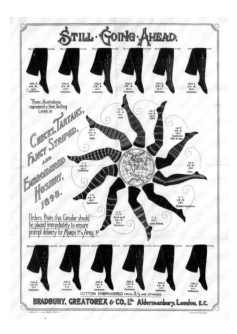

These illustrations represent a few Selling Lines in

CHECKS, TARTANS, FANCY STRIPED, AND EMBROIDERED HOSIERY, 1898.

Orders from this Circular should be placed immediately to ensure prompt delivery for MARCH 1st & APRIL 1st.

ALL ROUND THE WORLD

252½ E.
S.W., W.
14/11
Cashmere

270½ E.
S.W., W.
17/11
Cashmere.

283½ E.
S.W., W.
18/11
Cashmere.

284½ E.
S.W., W.
18/11
Cashmere.

291½ E.
S.W., W.
21/11
Cashmere.

293½ E.
S.W., W.
24/11
Cashmere.

91 F.
S.W., W.
9/11
Lisle.

101 F.
S.W., W.
10/11
Lisle.

102 F.
S.W., W.
10/11
Lisle.

119 F.
S.W., W.
19/11
Cashmere
Silk Stripe.

118 F.
S.W., W.
18/11
Lisle.

T. 9
S.W., W.
18/11
Cashmere

T. 9
S.W., W.
18/11
Cashmere

T. 7
S.W., W.
18/11
Ribbed Cashmere

T. 6
2 to 6
14/11 up 6
S.W., W.
16/11
Cashmere

T. 8
S.W., W.
18/11
Lisle Ribbed.

212½ E.
S.W., W.
7/11
Cashmere.

216½ E.
S.W., W.
8/11
Cashmere.

219½ E.
S.W., W.
9/11
Cashmere.
Camm 1

222½ E.
S.W., W.
10/11
Cashmere.
1 1 1

232½ E.
S.W., W.
12/11
Cashmere.

221½ E.
S.W., W.
9/11
Cashmere.

QUEEN VICTORIA

There were many ways in which manufacturers sought to associate their product with royalty, a practice which evolved during the reign of Queen Victoria. Apart from the official royal warrants which conferred the right to the magic phrase 'by appointment', shops claimed that they were patronized by royalty (in practice often minor royals) and manufacturers asserted that their products were used in the royal household. Products were often given names with a royal association: Sandringham, Osborne, Windsor, Victoria or Alexandra, for example.

However, it is the direct use of images of the monarch to promote products, usually under the pretext of celebrating a jubilee, which seems shocking today. The puns in both advertisements shown here associate themselves in a positive manner with the queen's long reign: 'the two safeguards of the constitution' for her Diamond Jubilee in 1897, and 'a "matchless" reign and a "matchless" metal polish' (*c.*1901).

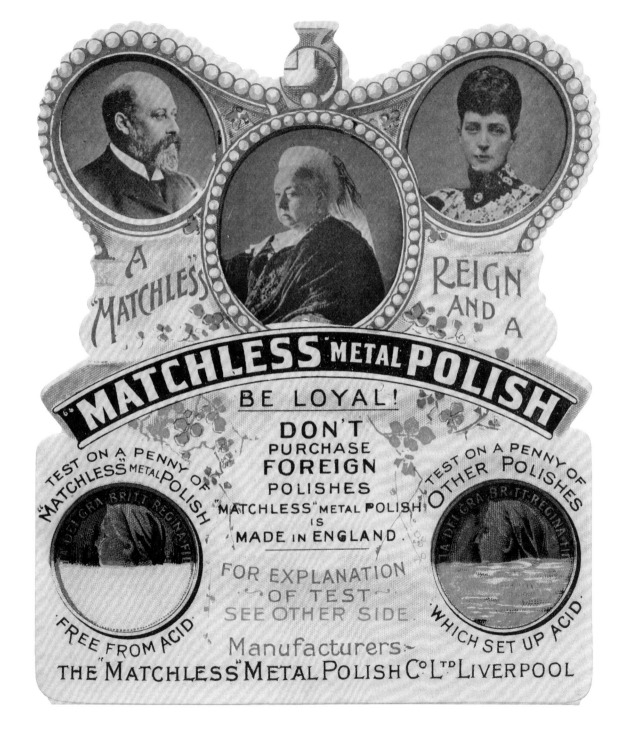

RAILWAYS

The railway network in Great Britain was crucial to the transportation of goods but also enabled people to travel significant distances for pleasure, including to the Continent by boat train from Charing Cross and Victoria.

The firm Arighi, Bianchi & Co., cabinet manufacturers, still in business today as Arighi Bianchi, was founded by two Italian immigrants in 1854 and relocated to its present location, part of the old silk mill near Macclesfield station, in 1883. The extension with its distinctive plate glass facade (based on Joseph Paxton's Crystal Palace) was built by George Roylance in 1892 and is now Grade II* listed. The proximity of the railway can be clearly seen in this bill heading, used in August 1898.

The history of W.H. Smith is inextricably linked to the heyday of the railway. Their first railway bookstalls opened in 1848 and the venture flourished, selling newspapers and popular fiction, notably yellowbacks (cheap reprints of out-of-copyright works) to a captive travelling public. From 1860, the firm expanded into printing, producing some of the iconic posters of the late nineteenth and early twentieth centuries. Their lucrative Railway Station Advertising System featured organized and prominent displays of posters. This brochure dates from the 1900s.

W·H·SMITH & SON'S RAILWAY STATION ADVERTISING SYSTEM

A Great Modern Business Force

OVER 4,000 STATIONS

W·H·SMITH & SON. 186. Strand, W.C.

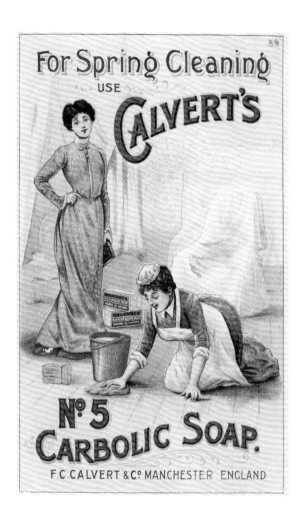

SERVANTS

The clearest indication of class in nineteenth- and twentieth-century advertising was the presence of servants. They were indispensable in the promotion of cleaning materials and are almost always shown 'upstairs', smiling, healthy, immaculate and willing, beside their benevolent mistress. This 1890s Calvert's advertisement for 'No. 5 Carbolic Soap' emphasizes more than most the subservience of the maid and the languid passivity of her employer.

Children are often shown with their nursemaids, but in *The Children's Party* (dating from the 1890s) they are also attended by the butler, while a delivery boy carries yet another box of Huntley & Palmers biscuits. There was a range of sweet biscuits specifically for children. Boxes of 'Nursery' and 'Littlefolk', can be seen here, as well as 'Supper'. This last may give the answer to the conundrum of the time shown on the clock (is it suppertime or lunchtime?).

Lutticke's small poster *Misery/Happiness* (overleaf) affords us a rare, if stylized, glimpse of a laundry in 1884, and the realities of steam and chapped hands.

THE CHILDREN'S PARTY.

MISERY

Heat, steam and overwork
Make the washing day a day of misery.

ELSINCK & WELSCH CHROM 34 WHITECROSS ST LONDON EC   MAKERS C HEARN & Co LONDON

HAPPINESS

THE EFFECT OF
LUTTICKE's ORIGINAL COLD WATER SOAP.
No heat, no steam, no chapped hands;
The washing done in one third of the time,
The best soap also for winter use.

SLOGANS

A good slogan is easily remembered and immediately evokes a brand name. Pears used a great many, often simultaneously. This one, 'He wont [sic] be happy 'till he gets it!', was parodied in more than one political cartoon. In this postcard, Kaiser Wilhelm II of Prussia reaches (unsuccessfully) for Europe. The slogan was also the title of a music hall song, dedicated to Messrs Pears. With words by Frank C. Burnard and music by Edward Solomons, it was sung nightly by George Stone in 1889 at the Gaiety Theatre in the burlesque *Faust Up to Date*. There were twelve verses!

SMOKING

Tobacco has been imported into Britain since 1565 and was first taxed in 1604. Tobacco and snuff were expensive products, accessible only to the rich. While snuff (a smokeless cured tobacco product) was inhaled by both sexes, smoking (of pipes, cigars and, later, cigarettes) was a male preserve. Cigarettes appeared from the 1830s, but were hand made and expensive. Machine-made cigarettes led to the commercialization of the industry in the 1880s.

Although some notorious bohemian women (such as George Sand) made a statement by smoking pipes in public as early as the 1830s, it was not until the 1890s that the 'new woman' adopted smoking as a symbol (alongside dress) of modern womanhood, challenging male prerogatives. This turn-of-the-century advertisement by the London tobacco manufacturer Martin Bros for dainty cigarettes for the female market ostensibly cites a fashionable journal as an authority. If such a journal existed, it has disappeared.

Carreras launched Craven "A" in 1921 – the first machine-made cork-tipped cigarette. In its marketing throughout the 1920s and 1930s, the firm claimed that the brand would not affect the throat. The war had democratized and officially condoned the smoking of cigarettes, with the inclusion of two ounces of tobacco a day in rations sent to the front by the government to boost morale. This aviator evokes the association of cigarettes with heroism.

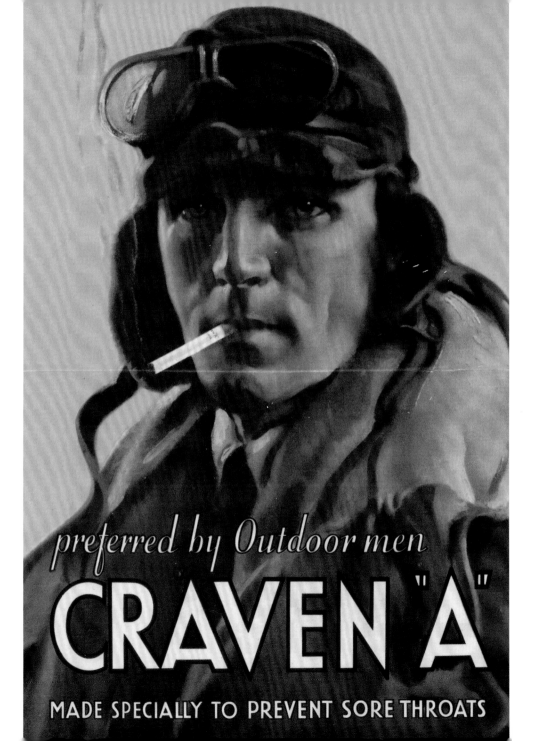

preferred by Outdoor men

CRAVEN "A"

MADE SPECIALLY TO PREVENT SORE THROATS

Brand loyalty was encouraged by competing cigarette manufacturers through the inclusion of collectible cards (often in series) in their packs. Taking their cue from the successful chromolithographed collectible cards of the meat extract manufacturer Liebig from the 1870s, cigarette cards cleverly engaged the juvenile public who, as suggested by this early twentieth-century comic postcard, would badger adults to buy cigarettes for the cards.

TECHNOLOGY

By the 1930s, the consumer was presented with a wealth of technology as well as domestic electrical gadgets.

Barr & Stroud, founded in 1888, initially specialized in optical rangefinders, but diversified during the First World War when they produced optical instruments for military purposes. Following a slump after the war, they turned their attention to civil instruments, including cinema projectors and binoculars, gaining a contract from the Royal Navy for the latter in 1930. The advertisement of 1937 (shown overleaf) beautifully captures the spirit of the time.

The Baird 'televisor' (p. 119) dates from 1933 and was marketed as 'the very latest marvel — television — the science of seeing by wire and wireless .... Not a photograph, nor yet a shadowgraph, but an actual moving image'.

The screen was small and broadcasting hours were short, but this represented nevertheless a gigantic step into the future.

EXTREMELY LIGHT &
BEAUTIFULLY FINISHED

BARR & STROUD
BINOCULARS

The BAIRD "TELEVISOR"

JOHN L. BAIRD
The famous Scottish Scientist, the Inventor of Television.

DURING the past quarter of a century Science has advanced in very rapid strides. We have seen the cinematograph, the aeroplane, wireless telegraphy and broadcasting come to perfection. In the latter part of the last century such developments were only dreamed of by writers of fiction; now we see them as accomplished facts.

The march of Science continues, however, and to-day the Baird Company presents to the public the very latest marvel—Television—the science of seeing by wire and wireless. It is an amazing thing, but none the less true, that a person sitting before the Baird transmitter can be seen thousands of miles away. Not a photograph, nor yet a shadowgraph, but an actual moving image of the subject being televised can be seen and heard in any home fitted with the Baird "Televisor" receiving apparatus.

The Baird "Televisor" reception set, which is of quite moderate dimensions, is as simple to operate as an ordinary wireless set.

With this set in your home you can sit in comfort and see the programmes broadcast by the B.B.C. And as the Baird Research Department, under the guidance of John L. Baird, develops the transmission of films, one may predict that the day is not far off when owners of the Baird Home Reception Set will be able to witness a whole film performance and hear a complete talkie in conjunction with their wireless set.

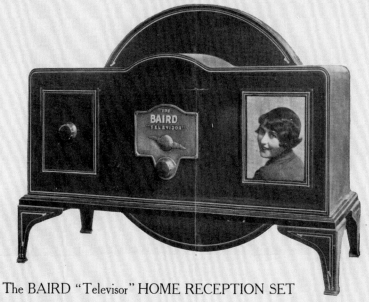

The BAIRD "Televisor" HOME RECEPTION SET

PRICE COMPLETE, FINISHED BROWN METAL CASING, ARTISTICALLY LINED
£26 - 5 - 0

BAIRD TELEVISION LIMITED
133, LONG ACRE, - LONDON, W.C.2

Telegrams: TELEVISOR, RAND, LONDON   'Phone: TEMPLE BAR 5401

DAILY BROADCAST OF
SOUND and VISION
by the
BAIRD PROCESS

Sound : 261 metres

Vision : 356 metres

MORNING TRANSMISSIONS
MONDAY, TUESDAY,
WEDNESDAY, THURSDAY,
and FRIDAY,
11 to 11.30 a.m.

EVENING TRANSMISSIONS
TUESDAYS and FRIDAYS
12 o'clock midnight till 12.30 a.m.

The programmes are published daily in the leading London and Provincial Newspapers.

TRADE CARDS AND TRADESMEN'S LISTS

Trade cards and tradesmen's lists provide the commercial and local historian with a wealth of textual and visual detail relating to trades and products.

Daniel Collins's trade card of c.1782 illustrates his wares and enumerates his trades. Funerals were performed by a surprising variety of tradesmen. Here the link is with the supply of coffins. The tents shown, with the royal monogram GR, are not mentioned in the engraved text, but relate to the military campaigns for which trunks were supplied.

The Grasshopper Tea Warehouse tradesman's list reveals a wide range of mostly imported pickles, sauces and fruits available in Newcastle upon Tyne in the mid-nineteenth century. Perhaps surprisingly, British wines are prominently promoted. Even if made from imported raisins, these were deemed preferable to the adulterations commonly sold as foreign wine.

TYPOGRAPHY

Advertising benefited from many typographic innovations, ranging from large, bold typefaces, which highlighted salient words, to ornamental type and typographic ornaments. Skilled printers made use of a combination of moveable type and wood-engraved lettering and images to push the boundaries. The two advertisements on pp. 122–3 use type with striking effect.

ROYAL ARCADE

Grasshopper TEA Warehouse.

BRITISH WINES.

GINGER	COWSLIP	TENT
ORANGE	ELDER	SHERRY
MALAGA	FRONTIGNAC	RED CURRANT
RASPBERRY	GOOSEBERRY	WHITE DITTO

PICKLES

Mushrooms
West India Pickles
Gorgona Anchovies
Red Cabbage
Cauliflower
Walnuts
French Beans
Onions
Picca'lla
Girkins
Capers

French Olives
Green Capsicums
Red Ditto
Mixed Pickles

SAUCES

Mushroom Ketchup and
 Powder
Walnut Ketchup
Burgess's Essence of
 Anchovies
Essence Gorgona Ditto

Acidulated Anchovy
 Sauce
Anchovy Paste
Lemon Pickle
Harvey's Sauce
Reading Sauce
Cevice
Indian Soy
Oyster Sauce
Lobster Sauce
Mogul Sauce
Sauce Royale
Prince Regent Sauce

Mullagatawny Paste
Bengal Chutny
Ditto Sauce
Currie Powder & Paste
Pate du Diable
Caviare and Tomata
Cayenne Pepper
Indian Currie Paste
Raspberry Vinegar
Chillie Ditto
Elder & Tarragona Do
French & British Ditto
Salad Oil, &c.

Fruits.

FRENCH PLUMS, in quarter Boxes, one-eighth Boxes, Cartons, half Cartons, and quarter Cartons
FRENCH PRUNES, in Barrels, half Barrels, quarter Barrels, and half Chests
MUSCATELL RAISINS, in Boxes, half Boxes, quarter Boxes, and Cartons
VALENTIA RAISINS, in Boxes and half Boxes
MALAGA RAISINS, in Frails, for Wine, &c.
BLACK SMYRNA DITTO, in Casks, for Ditto
RED SMYRNA DITTO, Ditto
SULTANA DITTO, in Drums
TURKEY FIGS, in Drums, half Drums, and quarter Drums
JORDAN, SHELL. VALENTIA, BARBARY, and BITTER ALMONDS
BARCELONA and MESSINA NUTS, NORMANDY PIPPINS, &c.

G. ATKINSON & CO.,   PRINTERS, DARLINGTON.

SOLD HERE by APPOINTMENT,

Patronised — Nobility,
BY THE — AND
Royal Family, — Gentry,

E. EWEN & SON'S,

Genuine Otto of Rose Soap,

(Prepaired from the Original Receipt;)

SUPERIOR

Emollient Old Brown,

WHITE, AND PINK

WINDSOR SOAP

Manufactured and Sold Wholesale only, by

E. EWEN & SON,

At their Wholesale Perfumery Warehouse, and Pink and Blue Saucer Manufactory,

17, Garlick Hill, Upper Thames Street, London.

QUICK, ENGRAVER AND PRINTER, BOWLING GREEN LANE, CLERKENWELL

E. Ewen & Son's early nineteenth-century window bill was a one-off, destined to be displayed in their shop, hence the elaborate hand-colouring and superior printing. Ewen proclaims that he is the sole vendor of his soap and that he is patronized by the royal family, the nobility and the gentry.

The BCM (Borough Cloth Mart) advertisement was printed by Giles Balne, formerly of Gye & Balne, in *c*.1831 and displays the innovative approach to typography and colour printing for which Balne was renowned, most notably in his bills and posters for Vauxhall Gardens.

U

UMBRELLAS

H. Johnston's umbrellas were famed in Belfast and were also favoured with a royal warrant. The shop, with its gold umbrella hanging outside, was easily recognizable. This intricately folded advertisement dates from the 1900s.

VERSE

The Co-operative Wholesale Society's *Jingles for Juveniles* uses the form of the limerick (popularized by Edward Lear) to promote its products while gently mocking the quintessential Edwardian society portrayed in Herbert Gill's charming illustrations.

WAR

The central theme of this elaborate 1890s Bovril
chromolithographed and die-cut mechanical work
was patriotism and the celebration of Britain's war
heroes. It shows (from left) Admiral of the Fleet Lord
Walter Kerr, Joseph Chamberlain, the marquess of

Salisbury and Field Marshal Frederick Roberts. There is just one phrase on the verso: 'Bovril a factor in our Empire's strength.'

The Boer Wars generated a large range of advertisements and were sufficiently remote geographically to have no effect on the availability of paper, unlike the First and Second World Wars. Sen-Sen was marketed as a 'breath perfume' and 'throat ease' until 2013. Its heyday was the 1930s, but the puzzle shown overleaf, complete with solution and free sample on the verso, dates from the Second Boer War (1899–1902).

With the First World War, women's dress lengths changed for ever, along with attitudes to women's capabilities. Flowing gowns gave way to utilitarian cuts and practical garments for the newly active woman who often worked outdoors. This Harrods folded sheet from 1917, while at the top of the price range, is nevertheless austere and uncompromisingly masculine, with references including 'man-tailored', 'military', 'trench', 'Field Service shades', 'men's coverts' and 'cavalry cut'.

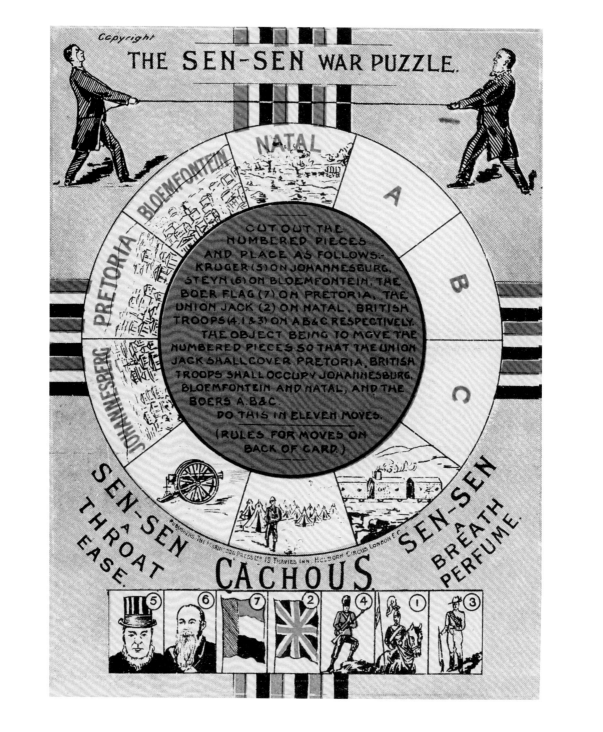

RULES FOR MOVING

THE OBJECT OF THE GAME — TO GET THE PIECES IN ORDER

  0   1   2   3   4   5 6 7

JOHANNESBURG PRETORIA BLOEMFONTEIN NATAL A B C

BY THE FOLLOWING RULES IN ELEVEN MOVES

     MOVE ONE PIECE AT A TIME BY JUMPING OVER ONE TO A
VACANT SPACE. NO PIECE MAY BE JUMPED OVER TWO OR MORE
OTHERS THAT ARE CLOSE TOGETHER. BUT MAY BE JUMPED OVER ANY
NUMB[...] VACANT SPACES BETWEEN THEM

SOLUTION

SOLVED IN THE FOLLOWING ELEVEN MOVES:—

7 TO THE CAMP	2 TO THE CANNON	4 TO NATAL
6 TO THE ARMOURED TRAIN	1 TO JOHANNESBURG	6 TO "B"
4 TO PRETORIA	3 TO BLOEMFONTEIN	2 TO PRETORIA
5 TO "A"	7 TO "C"	

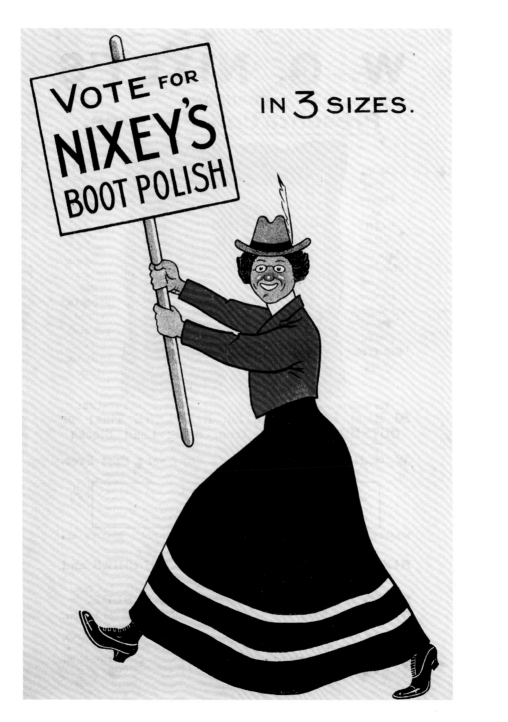

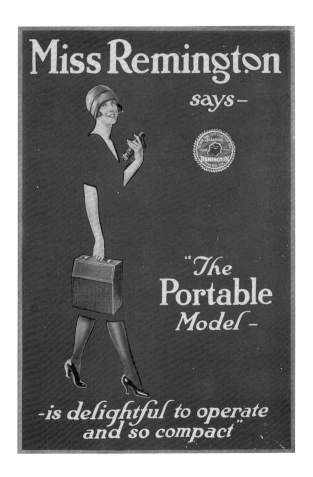

WOMEN

From the 1890s, women metamorphosed into stronger, more independent, freer 'new women'. Advertisers were quick to portray the symbols of this new freedom and its concomitant physical well-being: shorter skirts, the all-important bicycles (pp. 27–8) and a panoply of sports – golf, tennis, archery and skating, for example. By the 1930s, men were more frequently shown alongside women, no longer as protectors or evening companions but as partners in leisure activities and travel.

CHRISTMAS

The commercial elements of Christmas as we know it began in the Victorian era, including the first printed Christmas card (commissioned by Henry Cole from the artist John Callcott Horsley in 1842) and the shift to the giving of gifts on Christmas Day. While many gifts were modest, children of the rich were often given the latest toys.

Bon Marché was arguably the first purpose-built department store in Britain. It was inspired by, but unrelated to, the famous Paris store of the same name. The newly installed electric lighting in the basement meant that the store could stay open for longer.

TOYS & BAZAAR GOODS AT VERY SPECIAL PRICES.

1892–94

CHRISTMAS BAZAAR

THE BAZAAR WILL BE HELD IN THE SPACIOUS RECENTLY RENOVATED BASEMENT, NOW LIGHTED BY ELECTRICITY.

Fancy Goods of Every Description for Presents

Dolls, Toys & Games in Great Variety

A VISIT TO THE BON MARCHÉ WILL SUGGEST TO LADIES & GENTLEMEN THE MOST SUITABLE & ACCEPTABLE ◁ GIFTS ▷ FOR PRESENTATION AT CHRISTMAS AND THE NEW YEAR.

BON MARCHÉ BRIXTON LTD

NOW OPEN.

NOTE!—The BON MARCHÉ is very easy of access from all parts of London and Suburbs.

This modest four-page catalogue, with no illustrations other than that on the cover, lists the Christmas 'must-haves' for c.1892, with prices, under these headings: Dolls, games &c.; Trains & engines; Mechanical toys; Perfumery; Christmas crackers; Leather and fancy goods and Stationery; Fans; Christmas and New Year cards; and Christmas books and booklets. The last page is devoted to 'China & glass suitable for Xmas presents'. Although the abbreviation of Christmas to Xmas dates back at least to the 1750s, it was especially popular in advertising of the 1890s.

The small poster for Raphael Tuck is an example of 1930s nostalgia for a bygone age. At this time, Raphael Tuck was still a major publisher of calendars, greetings cards and books (especially gift books for children), but their heyday was in the 1890s and in the early days of the postcard at the dawn of the twentieth century.

YOUTH

Young children were frequently used by advertisers to suggest the purity of their product and for their 'cute' effect. They were often shown dwarfed by packaging, shop counters and policemen. Here John Hassall uses a camel to achieve the same effect, with gentle visual humour underlined by the pun.

The Gillette advertisement of c.1930, by contrast, eschews sentimentality. It makes its point that razors are safe enough for even a baby to use, but for today's viewer confronted with an oversized, chubby, somewhat unattractive baby filling the whole page and sporting a razor totally at odds with his tender age, the image is perhaps more shocking than reassuring.

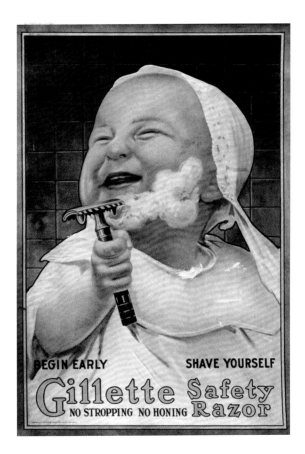

BEGIN EARLY   SHAVE YOURSELF

Gillette Safety Razor
NO STROPPING NO HONING

Z

ZEITGEIST

Advertisements encapsulate the zeitgeist through a combination of elements. Text, typography, layout, design, colour and illustrations all play a role in enabling us to situate the advertisement in a particular period.

The zeitgeist is perhaps seen most clearly through juxtapositions: the contrasting interiors shown in the Harlene and Hall's distemper advertisements (pp. 64–6), for example, or the very different conventions represented by the Fred Watts and Jantzen catalogues (pp. 29–31).

Occasionally, single images are sufficiently striking to convey a strong sense of period, for example Dudley Hardy's iconic image for the journal *To-Day* (p. 99) or the anonymous New Morris-Oxford Six poster (pp. 82–3).

Other advertisements are rooted in a particular period or relate to specific events or political movements, such as Bovril's free trade advertisement (p. 96) or Nixey's suffrage-related handbill (p. 130).

Our final image is one such. Barker & Spence's advertisement for their winter sale in January 1898, with its image of the prospector and its 'Yukon' pun, refers to the gold rush when 100,000 hopefuls went to the Yukon Valley in north-west Canada in search of 'Gold! Gold!! Gold!!!'.

GOLD! GOLD!! GOLD!!!

Why go to

KLONDYKE?

You have NOW a GOLDEN opportunity of picking up

PRECIOUS BARGAINS

— AT —

BARKER & SPENCE'S

GREAT

WINTER SALE.

"Yukon" depend upon getting Real Bargains here.

Ent. Sta. Hall.—C. N. & CO.

BARKER & SPENCE, High Street, Leamington.

These Prices include alteration of Name, Address, Date, &c., but Customers can have their own wording at an extra charge of 3/- per page or 10/- for the 4 pages, (any quantity.) THIS DESIGN is only supplied to one Establishment in a Town.

N.B.—A Poster (size 30 x 20) of this Figure can be had. The Figure is Printed in Red and Gold and Wording in Blue.
PRICES:—25, 11/-; 50, 13/6; 100, 18/0.

CLEMENTS, NEWLING & CO., 96, Wood Street, Cheapside, E.C.

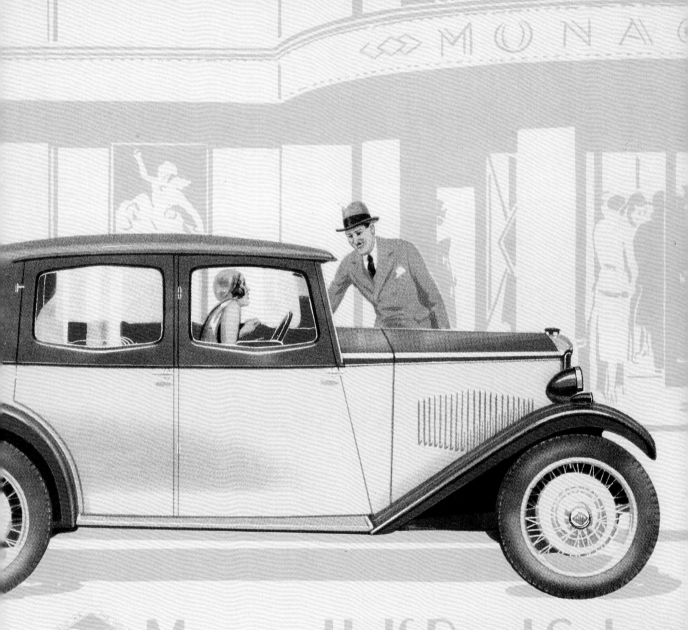

Riley Monaco Half-Panel Saloon
("Plus-Ultra" Series)

FURTHER READING

Flanders, J., *Consuming Passions: Leisure and Pleasure in Victorian Britain*, HarperPress, London, 2006.

Hudson, G., *The Design and Printing of Ephemera in Britain and America, 1720–1920*, British Library/Oak Knoll Press, London & New Castle, DE, 2008.

Iskin, R.E., *The Poster: Art, Advertising, Design, and Collecting, 1860s–1900s*, Dartmouth College Press, Hanover, NH, 2014.

Loeb, L.A., *Consuming Angels: Advertising and Victorian Women*, Oxford University Press, New York & Oxford, 1994.

Nevett, T.R., *Advertising in Britain: A History*, David & Charles, North Pomfret, VT, 1982.

Opie, R., *Remember When: A Nostalgic Trip through the Consumer Era*, Mitchell Beazley, London, 1999.

Twyman, M., *Printing 1770–1970: An Illustrated History of Its Development and Uses in England*, Eyre & Spottiswoode, London, 1970.

THE JOHN JOHNSON COLLECTION OF PRINTED EPHEMERA

The John Johnson Collection is one of the world's most important collections of printed ephemera — material that was not intended to survive its immediate purpose. The collection contains c.1.5 million items, spanning a broad range of British social and printing history. The strength of the collection lies in its eighteenth-, nineteenth- and early twentieth-century material. There is also a separate sequence, not yet fully available, of post-1960 ephemera.

Advertising forms one of eleven main sections, the other ten being: Artists; Authors; Booktrade and Publishing; Education; Entertainment; Political, Religious, Social and Economic History; Printing Processes; Private Presses; Transport and Travel. There are also ephemera kept by their form (bookmarks, menus, etc.). The c.1000 subdivisions include some fascinating headings, such as Umbrellas and Trunks, Printed on the Ice, and Woolly Whale (a private press).

Most of the Advertising material has been catalogued and digitized, and is available through the ProQuest platform: *The John Johnson Collection:* *An Archive of Printed Ephemera*. This is available free of charge in the UK (only) and through institutional subscription elsewhere. The project enables cross-searching of Advertising with four other sections: Booktrade; 19th-century Entertainment; Crime, Murders and Executions; and Popular Prints.

More information about the collection and its founder, John de Monins Johnson (1882–1956), can be found on the website, together with information about using the collection in person, and links to its various projects and finding aids.

Happy searching!

https://www.bodleian.ox.ac.uk/johnson

http://blogs.bodleian.ox.ac.uk/jjcoll/ (including a series of posts on advertising)

ProQuest project: http://johnjohnson.chadwyck.co.uk/geoLocSubscription.do (within UK)

http://johnjohnson.chadwyck.co.uk/ (outside UK, through institutional subscription only)

PICTURE CREDITS

All items, unless specified, are from the John Johnson Collection of Printed Ephemera (abbreviated to JJ),
© Bodleian Library, University of Oxford.

Introduction
Fig.1 JJ Beauty Parlour 1 (18)
Fig. 2 Bridgnorth Collection IV. G.117
Fig. 3 JJ Oil and Candles 3 (29)

A
Pears 'Bubbles': JJ Soap 6 (77a), (80b)
Sunlight: 'The Family Wash': JJ Soap 9 (61a)

B
Triumph Cycles (cover): JJ Bicycles box 6
Stower's Lime Cordial: JJ Soft Drinks 2 (23)

C
Fred Watts catalogue (pp. 4–5): JJ Advertising adds 1 (1)
Jantzens (open): JJ Women's Clothes and Millinery 6 (50a)
Kynoch: JJ Men's Clothes 6 (29)
Koko: JJ Beauty Parlour 2 (26b)
Abbey's Potash: JJ Patent Medicines 1 (1b)
Nelson Knife Polish: JJ Advertising adds folder (4)
Adams proof. JJ Advertising adds folder (1)
F. Allen & Sons: JJ Cocoa, Chocolate and Confectionery 1 (4b)
Cadbury's Cocoa: JJ Cocoa, Chocolate and Confectionery 1 (19)
Eureka Cooker: JJ Gas and Gas Appliances 1 (62)
Albionette: JJ Oil Lamps and Stoves 1 (6)
Adjusto corsets (p.11): JJ Women's Clothes and Millinery 1 (20)
Harness magnetic corsets: JJ Patent Medicines 17 (17)

D
Wynter's Glow: JJ Advertising artefacts adds (2)
Joseph Gillott's Peruvian Pen: JJ Labels 15 (4)

E
BTH Edison: JJ Electricity and Electrical Appliances 1
GEC Pavilion of Light (and pp. 6–7): JJ Electricity and Electrical Appliances 3

F
George Keith: JJ Ironmongery 1 (64)
Come into my kitchen: JJ Blotters 3

G
Pears 10 centime: JJ Advertising Arefacts adds (2) and JJ Soap 8* (6)
Priory Tea: JJ Tea and Coffee 3 (35)
Newball & Mason (and p. 10): JJ Tea and Coffee 6 (40)
Bournville Quoits: JJ Advertising adds 1 (6)

H
Andrews Liver Salt postcard: JJ John Hassall box
Washable beaver hat: JJ Hats 1 (18)
Sale of artistic millinery: JJ Window Bills and Advertisements 9 (27)
Worm-Plaister: JJ Patent Medicines 18 (5)
Carbolic Smoke Ball: JJ Patent Medicines 8 (42a)
Mother Seigel's Syrup: JJ Patent Medicines 6 (19)

I
Harlene: JJ Beauty Parlour 2 (7b), (9)
Hall's Distemper: JJ Oil and Candles 2 (17b)

J
Hudson's poster: JJ Window Bills and Advertisements folder 5 (4)
Sunday at Home, June 1889 (pp. 4–5): JJ Advertisers: Sunday at home 2
West End Review (Mucha) (and p. 14): JJ Prospectuses of Journals 52 (5a)
Pall Mall Budget: JJ Prospectuses of Journals 40 (53c)

K
Rowntree's Coronation Souvenir: JJ Advertising Adds 1 (15)
Lewis and Burrows' All loyal subjects: JJ Patent Medicines 14 (29)
GEC Coronation Celebrations (pp. 14–15): JJ Electricity and Electrical Appliances 3

INDEX